STAAR

SUCCESS STRATEGIES

Grade 4
Writing

STAAR Test Review for the
State of Texas Assessments of Academic Readiness

Dear Future Exam Success Story:

Congratulations on your purchase of our study guide. Our goal in writing our study guide was to cover the content on the test, as well as provide insight into typical test taking mistakes and how to overcome them.

Standardized tests are a key component of being successful, which only increases the importance of doing well in the high-pressure high-stakes environment of test day. How well you do on this test will have a significant impact on your future- and we have the research and practical advice to help you execute on test day.

The product you're reading now is designed to exploit weaknesses in the test itself, and help you avoid the most common errors test takers frequently make.

How to use this study guide

We don't want to waste your time. Our study guide is fast-paced and fluff-free. We suggest going through it a number of times, as repetition is an important part of learning new information and concepts.

First, read through the study guide completely to get a feel for the content and organization. Read the general success strategies first, and then proceed to the content sections. Each tip has been carefully selected for its effectiveness.

Second, read through the study guide again, and take notes in the margins and highlight those sections where you may have a particular weakness.

Finally, bring the manual with you on test day and study it before the exam begins.

Your success is our success

We would be delighted to hear about your success. Send us an email and tell us your story. Thanks for your business and we wish you continued success-

Sincerely,

Mometrix Test Preparation Team

TABLE OF CONTENTS

Top 15 Test Taking Tips

1. Know the test directions, duration, topics, question types, how many questions
2. Setup a flexible study schedule at least 3-4 weeks before test day
3. Study during the time of day you are most alert, relaxed, and stress free
4. Maximize your learning style; visual learner use visual study aids, auditory learner use auditory study aids
5. Focus on your weakest knowledge base
6. Find a study partner to review with and help clarify questions
7. Practice, practice, practice
8. Get a good night's sleep; don't try to cram the night before the test
9. Eat a well balanced meal
10. Wear comfortable, loose fitting, layered clothing; prepare for it to be either cold or hot during the test
11. Eliminate the obviously wrong answer choices, then guess the first remaining choice
12. Pace yourself; don't rush, but keep working and move on if you get stuck
13. Maintain a positive attitude even if the test is going poorly
14. Keep your first answer unless you are positive it is wrong
15. Check your work, don't make a careless mistake

Writing Assessment

Composition

Drafting a paper

When beginning to write, you should develop a plan about what you want to discuss and the points you want to make. An outline can prove helpful if you are writing a nonfiction piece. If you are writing a narrative, you might want to make a story map. Next, you should write a first draft. Once you have finished the writing, you should put it aside for a time. When you come back to it, you will see it with fresh eyes and will see more easily what needs to be changed or revised. After you make the revisions and put the writing aside again, then reread the writing and begin to edit it for any grammatical, spelling, punctuation, or usage errors. Make sure that the supporting details are clear and in a logical order in a report. Rework the dialogue to make it more precise in a story. Read your work to someone else and ask for feedback. Finally, revise it again.

Main idea and topic sentence

A paragraph should be unified around a main point. A good topic sentence summarizes the paragraph's main point. A topic sentence is more general than subsequent supporting sentences are. Sometime the topic sentence will be used to close the paragraph if earlier sentences give a clear indication of the direction of the paragraph. Sticking to the main point means deleting or omitting unnecessary sentences that do not advance the main point. The main point of a paragraph deserves adequate development, which usually means a substantial paragraph. A paragraph of two or three sentences often does not develop a point well enough, particularly if the point is a strong supporting argument of the thesis. An occasional short paragraph is fine, particularly if it is used as a transitional device. A choppy appearance should be avoided.

Supporting details

Example
Read the following main idea of a story and write a supporting detail for it:
     Madison's favorite thing to talk about was strawberries.

A good supporting detail would need to include information that supports or explains more about the main idea. A supporting detail might read: "She also loved to eat them," or "She also grew strawberries in her backyard." Supporting details provide additional information about the main idea that has not already been presented to the reader. A supporting detail further develops the topic of the story and provides an explanation of a part of the main idea.

In the example supporting details above, note that the topic is still focused on the subject of strawberries and action that the character takes in relation to that particular subject. A main idea will often appear in the first one to two paragraphs of a story. Supporting details appear later in a paragraph or in other paragraphs within the story.

Fact vs. opinion

A fact is something that is true. For example, "The capital of Texas is Austin." This is a true statement because it is something that can be proved. An opinion is an idea that some people might agree with, but other people might not. For example, "It is fun to sing." Some people might agree with that statement, but others might not. It is not a fact because it cannot be proved.

An author may try to persuade a reader about something. The author might use many opinions and might not use many facts. It is important for the reader to be able to tell the difference between a fact and an opinion. When a reader reads a statement but is not sure if it is a fact or an opinion, the reader should ask, "Can this be proved?" If it can, it is a fact. If it cannot, it is an opinion.

Conclusion

While a good beginning is essential, equally important to an essay, lecture, or other presentation is an effective conclusion. A good concluding statement should sum up the overall intention of the text and serve to "wrap up" the presentation so the reader is aware that you have made a logical ending to your thesis and has closure. Ideally the conclusion would review the most important points made in the presentation, the reasoning employed, and the supporting arguments for this reasoning. The conclusion builds a bridge between the presentation and the audience that helps to reassert the importance of the effort and impact the viewer's memory favorably. A good conclusion allows the reader to sit back and weigh the overall impact of the presentation.

Purpose

A purpose is the reason that an author writes. It is why the author writes an article. There are many reasons to write articles. An author may write about ideas on a subject. The author might write a letter to the editor. An author may write to problem-solve. There might be instructions on how to do something. An author may write to inform. An author may want to explain something. An author might want to describe something. An author may want to tell a story. An author may write to make a reader laugh. An author may write a story that makes a reader sad. These are some of the purposes that authors have.

<u>Example</u>
>Spray a nonstick pan with oil.
>Put the pan on a burner.
>Turn it on medium heat.
>Break two eggs into a bowl.
>Beat them until mixed.
>Pour the egg mixture into the pan.
>Stir the eggs slowly until they set.
>Serve with toast or home fries

This passage looks like a list. This list has instructions. They are in the order in which they must be done. The instructions say to spray a nonstick pan with oil. It says to put the pan on a burner and turn it on medium heat. It says to break two eggs into a bowl and mix them. It says to pour the eggs into the pan. It says to stir them until they set. It says to serve the eggs with toast or home fries. The passage is a recipe. It tells how to make something. That is the purpose of the passage. It tells the reader how to make scrambled eggs. It instructs the reader about how to make an egg dish.

Personal voice

Some stories have a personal voice. This personal voice is the author's individual viewpoint. A personal voice helps make a story interesting. The individual voice tells how an author feels about what is happening. It tells the reader what the author thinks about the events in a story. The voice helps the reader understand the author. The voice helps the reader figure out why the story is being told. The voice makes the story meaningful to the reader. An author can let a reader know what the author feels by giving clues. One clue is the use of mood. Another is the use of tone. A personal voice can be in the first person. This means the author uses the pronoun "I." A personal voice can be in the third person. This means the author uses the pronoun "he" or "she."

<u>Example</u>

> It was my birthday and I didn't know what to expect. I woke up early and went downstairs. Mom had pancakes cooking, my favorite food. "Good morning, Billy," she said. She gave me a big hug and said, "Happy Birthday." That made me smile. Then she handed me a box. It was wrapped and had a ribbon. I was excited. I opened it quickly. Inside there was a pair of ice skates. It was just what I wanted. I kissed my mother and went to show my friend Bryan.

To identify a personal voice you need to look for clues. The reader needs to see what the personal voice says and how it acts. The reader needs to figure out who the personal voice is. In this passage, the personal voice has a mother. She cooks him breakfast. She cooks him his favorite food. She calls him Billy, so the reader can tell he is a boy. He is probably young if his mother cooks him breakfast. He smiles, so he seems happy. He is also excited because he has a present. The personal voice is pleased with the present. The reader knows this because the voice says so.

Revision

There are many ways to revise writing. One way is to check for the logic of ideas. Another way is to make sure there is cohesion. This means that everything in the writing belongs together. There must also be a progression of ideas. This means that one idea should fit naturally with another. After the writing is done, there are other ways to revise it. Sometimes sentences need to be rearranged. Sometimes sentences need to be deleted. Sometimes sentences need to be added. Sometimes sentences need to be combined. The best way to revise writing is to reread it carefully, and ask whether the writing makes sense. Ask if the writing flows well. Ask what can be added or deleted.

Making sentences more distinct

Choose the way in which the following sentence could be made less vague:
    Terri and Jim heard a noise outside.
A. Change Terri and Jim to "They."
B. Change heard to "were hearing."
C. Change noise to "screech."
D. Change outside to "somewhere."

The correct choice is C. "Terri and Jim heard a screech outside." The word *noise* is too general, and could mean any number of different sounds. The word *screech* is specific. It describes the kind of noise that Terri and Jim heard. It tells the reader that the noise was a high pitched, urgent cry. Choice A would leave the statement even more vague. *They* is a pronoun that could replace *Terri and Jim*, but the reader would not know who "they" refers to. Choice B only changes the tense and does not improve the sentence. Choice D makes the statement more vague since it doesn't help the reader know where the noise was heard.

Editing sentences to read better

Describe how to edit this sentence so it will read better:
    Teresa likes to play ice hockey one day she hit the puck hard. She hoped ot would be her first goal. The refere she thought, and the referee called for a face-off. The puck bounced off the goalpost, into the stands.

Teresa likes to play ice hockey. One day, she hit the puck hard. It is going to be my first goal, she thought. But the puck bounced off the goalpost and into the stands. The referee called for a face-off.
The first sentence is too long and needs to be broken into separate thoughts. "Teresa likes to play ice hockey." Hitting the puck and thinking it could be a goal is awkward and needs to be re-worded. There should be a pause after "One day," so a comma is needed. The idea that it could be her first goal is clearer by changing the tense. "It is going to be" rather than "it was." The referee calling for a face-off after the puck bounced off the goal becomes the last sentence.

Connecting sentences

The following example shows how to choose the best way to connect the sentences:

> Penny brought cookies to the party. Her brother brought chocolate milk to the party.

A. Penny brought cookies to the party, or her brother brought chocolate milk.
B. Penny brought cookies to the party, if her brother brought chocolate milk.
C. Penny brought cookies to the party, before her brother brought chocolate milk.
D. Penny brought cookies to the party, and her brother brought chocolate milk.

Choice D is correct. The two ideas are alike, so they are joined with "and." Also, the repeated words "to the party" do not have to be repeated. A is in correct. There is no choice between the two thoughts. B is not correct. The ideas are not different, C is incorrect. There is no element of time between the two ideas.

Adding, moving, and deleting sentences

A paragraph is a group sentences. The sentences are about one main idea. All of the sentences should support the main idea. The sentences should be arranged in an order that makes sense. There should be a topic sentence that tells the main idea. The other sentences should support the main idea. After writing a first draft, the writer should go back and read each paragraph carefully. If a sentence does not support the main idea, it should be deleted. Or, if the writer thinks that more information is needed to support the main idea, another sentence should be added.

Example 1

Identify which sentence should be deleted from the passage below:

> (1) Bonnie got a camera for her birthday. (2) It was her very first camera, and she was very excited. (3) She put in the batteries and the memory card and walked over to the window. (4) The zoo has a new panda. (5) She looked through the monitor and took her very first picture. (6) She ran out to show the picture to her mother.

This paragraph is about Bonnie getting her first camera for her birthday. That is the main idea. Sentences 1 and 2 tell the reader this. Sentence 3 tells what Bonnie did. She put the batteries and memory card into the camera and then walked to the window. This sentence has supporting information about the main idea. Sentences 5 and 6 also tell the reader what she did with her camera. These sentences support the main idea. Sentence 5 does not talk about the main idea. It says that the zoo has a new panda. This has nothing to do with the main idea. It should be deleted.

Example 2

Identify which sentence should be moved to the end of the passage below:

> (1) Chip and his dad were going to go fishing today. (2) The got the rods and the tackle box and put them in the car. (3) Chip pulled hard and reeled the fish into the net. (4) They drove to the pond, got into the boat and rowed out to the center. (5) In just a few minutes, Chip felt a pull on his rod.

This paragraph is about Chip and his dad going fishing. It tells all of the events in the order that they happened. It starts out saying that Chip and his dad were going fishing and that they got the rods and the tackle box and put them in the car. But sentence 3 jumps ahead. It is not in the right place. The paragraph then goes on to say that they drove to the pond and got into the boat. After they rowed to the center of the pond, Chip felt a pull on his rod. Sentence 3 tells what happened next. So it should be moved to the end of the paragraph. It is the conclusion of the paragraph.

<u>Example 3</u>
Identify which sentence should be added to the passage below:
> Denise and her parents always went to visit her grandmother on Thanksgiving. They always took the train. She loved riding on the train. She also loved her grandmother's cooking. Denise knew the time was getting close to Thanksgiving because the class was drawing pictures of pilgrims in school.

A. She loved going to the circus with her parents and her best friend.
B. The next day her mother said she had bought the train tickets.
C. Next week they were going to go to Disneyland.
D. There was a big traffic jam on the way to the airport.

Choice B is the correct answer. This sentence fits in best with the passage. The passage says that Denise and her parents always took the train to see her grandmother and that Denise loved to ride on the train. Choice B says Denise's mother said that she had bought the train tickets. This is connected to the idea of going by train to see her grandmother. Choices A, C, and D do not relate to the passage. There was nothing in the passage about the circus, Disneyland, or going to the airport. So they are all incorrect.

Combining sentences

Identify which sentences should be combined in the passage below:
> (1) Eddie wanted to make a birthday card for his mom. (2) He got some paper. (3) He folded it so it was like a card. (4) Later in the day, he drew a picture of some flowers on the front of the card. (5) Just before he gave his mom the card, he wrote "Happy Birthday Mom" on the inside

This passage is about Eddie wanting to make a birthday card for his mom. It tells how Eddie got some paper. It says he folded the paper so it was like a card. It also says that he drew a picture of some flowers on the card. It ends by saying that he wrote "Happy Birthday Mom and that we was going to give it to her tonight. Sentences 2 and 3 should be combined into one sentence. "He got some paper and he folded it so it was like a card." Replacing two simple sentences with one compound one makes the passage read more smoothly.

Editing

Editing

Editing has many purposes. One important purpose is to make sure that standard English is being used. This means checking to see if the verb tenses are correct and if the verbs agree with their subject. This also means checking for other grammatical mistakes including the correct use of punctuation and spelling. Pronouns need to be checked so the correct form is used and pronoun antecedents or referents must be checked to see if they agree with each other. Another main purpose of editing is to ensure that there are varied sentences used and that the writing flows from one idea to another. Again, an editor would look for the appropriate word choices to make the writing more specific and engaging.

Example 1
Tell how the reader should edit the passage below:

> Our puppy was having fun. He was running jumping, and chewing on toz. I was watching him play in the yard? Our puppys' name is oscar. Why did we name him that! It was the name that my little brother wanted.

There are several corrections that should be made to the passage. First there should be a comma after running. This is a series and the words need to be separated by commas. The word "toz" is misspelled. It should be "toys." The third sentence is not a question. It is a statement. It should have a period not a question mark. The word "puppys'" is an incorrect possessive form. It should be "puppy's." Proper names are always capitalized, so "oscar" should be "Oscar." The next to the last sentence is a question. It should end in a question mark, not an exclamation mark.

Example 2
Proofread and correct the following sentences:

> I had a little black Cocker Spaniel once. His name was lucky. One time he came to my door, and scratched. He did'nt bark he just scratched. When I opened the door I saw he had my sisters toy doll he wanted to play.

In the first sentence, a comma should be inserted after *little* since adjectives in a series need to be separated by commas. In the second sentence the proper name *Lucky* should be capitalized, since it is the dog's name. The comma in sentence three should be deleted. It is not needed. In the fourth sentence the contraction is misspelled. It should be *didn't.* In the fifth sentence there should be an apostrophe in the word *sister's* since it shows possession. There is also a run-on sentence in the fifth sentence. There should be a period after doll and the word *He* should be capitalized since it is the first word of a sentence.

Example 3
Identify which word could be substituted for the underlined word in the sentence below to make the sentence more precise.

Birds of paradise are usually colorful birds, although some are <u>plain</u>.
A. boring
B. uninteresting
C. dull
D. drab

Choice D is the best answer. This word is much more precise than *plain* is, and it gives the reader a better idea of just what the birds look like. Choice A, *boring,* isn't a good word to describe a bird. Both choice B and C are possible answers, but they are not as precise as the word *drab* is and wouldn't give as clear a picture of the birds that are not colorful.

<u>Example 4</u>
Choose the best word to substitute for the underlined word in the passage below and explain why it is the best choice.

> Sheila had been standing by the bus stop for nearly a half-hour. It was raining hard now and she was getting <u>wet</u>. Her hair was dangling over her eyes and her coat was completely soaked. She tried to seek shelter under a canopy, but there was no room left.

A. drenched
B. damp
C. moist
D. sprayed

Sheila's hair "is dangling over her eyes" and her coat "is completely soaked." She is more than just wet so this word is inadequate. The best word to substitute for the word *wet* is choice A, *drenched.* She is really, really wet and this word is much more precise than *wet,* since it suggests she was soaked through. Choice B could not be substituted, since *damp* means only a little wet, and neither C nor D is a good choice either, since *moist* means a little wet also; there is no mention of her being *sprayed,* so that is incorrect as well.

Verbs

Verbs state what happens (such as eat or run) or describe a state of being (such as be or appear). All verbs indicate time (hear, heard, will hear; is, was, will be).

All verbs need a subject identifying who or what is acting or being- I think; I am.

Some verbs also have a direct object (He eats meat).

Verbs have five forms: base form, past tense, past participle, present participle, infinitive.

Regular verbs form the past tense and the past participle by adding -ed to the base form of the verb (kick, kicked, kicked; walk, walked, walked).

Irregular verbs form the past tense and past participle in many different ways: buy, bought, bought; see, saw, seen.

Nouns

Nouns name things--persons, places, actions or ideas. Nouns are subjects, direct objects, indirect objects, objects of prepositions, predicate complements and predicate nouns. Nouns also show possession. Most nouns name things that can be counted-one potato, two potatoes, three potatoes. Most count nouns are concrete nouns. They name things that can be touched, seen, smelled, heard, tasted-table, movie, flower, song, candy bar. A/an are used with singular count nouns. "The" is used with both singular and plural count nouns.

Collective count nouns identify groups-family, team, herd, crowd, class. Although these nouns represent a group of individuals, they are understood as one unit and take a singular verb. When they represent two or more groups, they are plural. Most count nouns form the plural by adding "s" Example: toe-toes. Irregular count nouns form the plural in a variety of ways: count nouns ending in "s, sh, x, or z" add "es"; some count nouns change forms; some count nouns stay the same. Non-count nouns name things that can't be counted. Follow these rules. Never add "s" to a non-count noun; always use a singular verb; never use a/an with a non-count noun; never use many with a non-count noun.

Transition words

The use of appropriate transition words helps to clarify the relationships between ideas and concepts and creates a more cohesive passage. A good writer knows that such words and phrases serve to indicate the relationship between ideas and concepts. Words or phrases that show causality between ideas include "as a result," "consequently" and "therefore." Words that show a compare-and-contrast relationship include "however," "on the other hand," "in contrast" and "but." When introducing examples of different concepts, words such as "namely," "for example" and "for instance" act as transition words. Transition words such as "foremost," "primarily," "secondly," "former" and "latter" can be used when showing the order of importance of ideas or concepts.

Correct spelling

Words must be spelled correctly so that the reader can properly understand what the writer is saying. For example, in the sentence "We are going to go today to see a siens exhibit today about the moon," there is no way of understanding what the writer means by "siens." Is it silent? That does not make any sense. Is it signs? That does not make much sense either. Or is it science? That would make more sense. "We are going to see a science exhibit today about the moon." So it is very important to re-read what you write and check the spelling before turning in a final draft.

Special cases for spelling

The English language has many special cases when it comes to spelling. Some examples are given below:

Double consonant
There are a few simple rules to follow when trying to decide whether to use a double consonant or not. If a word ends in a consonant-vowel-consonant pattern, it gets a double consonant +*ed* or *ing*. So the word *stop* becomes *stopped*, and the word *hop* becomes

hopping. A two-syllable word where the emphasis is on the second syllable will also get a double consonant +*ed* or *ing.* So the word *refer* becomes *referred*, and the word *begin* becomes *beginning.*

<u>Ways to spell *sh*</u>
The *sh* sound can be spelled several different ways. For example it could be -sion, -tion, or -cian. After the letters *l, r,* and *s* use *sion.* Examples include the words *version, mission,* and *compulsion.* After any other letter it is *tion,* except occasionally after an *n.* Examples include *fraction, nation, mention,* and *pension.* If it describes an occupation then it gets *cian.* Examples of this are *politician, magician,* and *physician.*

<u>Silent letters</u>
Silent letters are letters in words that are not pronounced, like the *k* in *knee.* There are some rules for identifying silent letters, but like with most rules in the English language there are exceptions. It is also difficult because more than 60% of English words have a silent letter. A few of the more common rules are as follows:

Silent B- The *b* is silent when preceded by an *m* at the end of a word.
Examples: climb, bomb
It is often silent when followed by a *t,* but not always.
Examples: debt, doubt
Exception: obtain
Silent K- The *k* is silent when followed by an *n.*
Examples: knife, knee, knot
Silent N- The *n* is silent when preceded by an *m.*
Examples: autumn, column
Silent GH- The *gh* is silent when followed by a *t.*
Examples: night, bought
Silent H- The *h* may be silent when preceded by a *p, g,* or *ex.*
Examples: shepherd, ghost, exhausted
It may also be silent when it comes between two vowels.
Example: vehicle
Silent S- An *s* is silent when followed by an *l.*
Examples: island, aisle
Silent W- The *w* is silent when followed by an *r* at the beginning of a word.
Examples: write, wrong

<u>Homophones</u>
A homophone is a word that is pronounced the same as another word but has a different meaning. It can be spelled the same as the other word or it can be spelled differently. It is important to be able to distinguish which form of the word is being used so it can be spelled correctly. In the case of *there, they're,* and *their,* all three words have different meanings and must be used appropriately. The word *there* represents a place, while the word *they're* is a contraction for the words *they are,* and the word *their* is used to show possession.

Double negatives

A double negative is when a speaker uses two "no" type words in one sentence. In English, double negatives are incorrect. Negative words include *no, none, nothing, no one, nobody* and *never.* Negative verbs use the word *not.* The rule is that if you use a negative word in a sentence, you cannot use a negative verb too. "He has not never been late to school" is incorrect. It can be corrected in two ways, since there are two negatives. "He has never been late to school" or "He has not ever been late to school" are correct. The same is true of verb contractions. For example *can't* is a contraction for *cannot.* "Betty can't do nothing right today." This sentence has a double negative: *can't* and *nothing.* It needs to be corrected. "Betty can't do anything right today" or "Betty can do nothing right today" are correct.

Parts of speech

There are eight parts of speech. A verb is the action word. It can also tell the state-of-being of a person, animal or thing. A noun is a person, place or thing. A pronoun is a word used in place of a noun. An adjective describes a noun or pronoun. An adverb describes a verb, adjective or another adverb. A preposition is a word that relates its object to another word in the sentence. A conjunction joins two ideas together in a sentence. An interjection shows feelings. Sentences with interjections often end with an exclamation mark. An interjection can stand alone such as "Ouch!"

Adjectives and adverbs

An adjective is a word that describes a noun or pronoun. "She has a little dog." In this sentence the word *little* is an adjective. It describes the dog. Adjectives make writing clearer and more interesting. So do adverbs. An adverb describes a verb, an adjective, or another adverb. "Mandy drove slowly." In this sentence the word *slowly* is an adverb. It modifies the verb *drove.* It tells the reader how Mandy was driving, slowly. An adverb can tell how, when, where and to what extent. "He drove really fast." In this sentence, the adverb *really* describes the adjective *fast* and tells the reader how quickly he drove. "We like to cook out quite often." In this sentence, *quite* is an adverb. It describes another adverb, *often.*

Comparative and superlative adjectives
When the writer compares two nouns the writer uses a comparative adjective. A comparative adjective is formed by adding an –er to the word. For instance the comparative form of the adjective "tall" is "tall*er*." Jerry is tall*er* than Byron. The word "than" is usually used with a comparative adjective. Superlative adjectives are used when comparing three or more nouns. The superlative form of an adjective is often formed by adding -*est* to the adjective. Jerry is the tall*est* in class. Another way to form a superlative adjective is to use the word "most" in front of the adjective. Lillian is the *most* careful of all the children.

Prepositional phrase

A prepositional phrase has a preposition and an object. The object comes at the end of this kind of phrase. It shows relationships. "Connie sat behind her sister." In this sentence the prepositional phrase is "behind her sister." The preposition *behind* shows the relationship between Connie and her sister. Prepositional phrases can be used at the start of a sentence. They can be in the middle of a sentence. They can also be at the end of a sentence. A writer uses this kind of phrase to make writing more descriptive. "The dog watched us." With a prepositional phrase the sentence is less vague. "The dog with very large, brown eyes watched us."

<u>Example</u>
Identify the sentence that contains a prepositional phrase.
A. We can play outside or we can watch TV.
B. Terry searched everywhere for his sneakers.
C. He poured the lemonade very slowly.
D. Chris wrote a poem and showed his teacher.

Choice B is the correct answer. "His sneakers" is the object of the preposition "for." "For his sneakers" is a prepositional phrase. A is a compound sentence joined with "or." C is a simple sentence with the adverb "very slowly" modifying the verb. D is also a compound sentence, joined by "and."

Pronouns

Pronouns are used to replace nouns. They substitute for a person, place or thing. "Tommy is running home. He is running home." In these sentences the pronoun *he* takes the place of *Tommy*. Some pronouns are subject pronouns. They are: *I, you, he, she, it, we,* and *they*. There are also object pronouns. They are: *me, you, him, her, it, us,* and *them*. Possessive pronouns are used to show that someone or something owns something. Some possessive pronouns are used before a noun, such as *my, your, his, her, its, our,* and *their*. Some possessive pronouns stand alone. They are: *mine, yours, his, hers, ours,* and *theirs*. Pronouns must always agree with the noun that they refer to. "Peter and Lucy took their seats in the front row." In this sentence, the possessive pronoun *their* refers to the plural subject *Peter and Lucy*. A reflexive pronoun occurs when the pronoun is after the noun that is in the sentence. Reflexive pronouns are: *myself, herself, ourselves,* and *himself*.

<u>Example</u>
Identify which sentence uses a pronoun incorrectly and tell why it is incorrect:
A. Dad said Willie and I could mow lawns this summer.
B. The neighbors always let its dog chase after the mailman.
C. A family of little chicks followed Larry and him around.
D. Jenny said earlier today that her book is on the shelf.

The correct choice is B. This sentence does not use a pronoun correctly. A pronoun must always agree with the noun that it refers to. In choice B, the possessive pronoun *its* is singular. The noun it refers to is plural, *neighbors*. A plural pronoun needs to be used instead. The plural possessive form is *their*. "The neighbors always let their dog chase after the mailman." This sentence is now correct. Choice A is correct and uses the subject pronoun *I* correctly. Choice C uses a correct form of the object pronoun *him*. Choice D uses the correct possessive pronoun *her*, since it refers to the subject Jenny.

<u>Objective case pronouns</u>
An objective pronoun is a pronoun that is the object of a verb. The objective pronouns are: *me, you, him, her, it, us,* and *them*. For example in the sentence "Monica invited us to her birthday party," "us" is the objective pronoun. It is the object of the verb "invited." Objective pronouns can be used in compound sentences as well: "Monica invited Jane and us to her birthday party." Here the object of the verb is "Jane and us." Objective pronouns can be used with a preposition: "His sister pulled the blanket over me." In this case "me" is the object of the preposition "over."

Conjunctions

Sentences can be joined together by using conjunctions. *And, but,* and *or* are some conjunctions. Each conjunction has a different meaning. If two ideas are alike, join them together with *and.* "Paul mowed the grass. Jeff trimmed the shrubs." These ideas are alike. "Paul mowed the grass, and Jeff trimmed the shrubs." If the ideas are different, use *but.* "The dishes looked clean. They were still dirty." "The dishes looked clean, but they were dirty." If there is a choice between ideas, use *or.* "You can help with the dishes. You can make your bed." These ideas offer a choice. "You can help with the dishes, or you can make your bed."

Example
Choose which conjunction should be used in the sentence and explain why:
        Susie wanted to play outside, ___ her mother said it was too rainy.
A. and
B. or
C. but
D. so

A conjunction joins one part of a sentence to another. Conjunctions show the relationship between the two parts of a sentence. They can show how the parts of the sentence are alike. They can show a result. They can show how the parts of a sentence are different. If the reader tries each one of the conjunction in the empty line, the reader can see which one makes the most sense. "And" does not make sense. This is not the correct relationship between the two parts of the sentence. These ideas are not alike. If the reader tries "or" or "so," the sentence doesn't make sense either. "Or" is used to give a choice between two ideas. "So" shows that something is a result of the first idea. The correct conjunction is "but." It joins two ideas that are different. This conjunction makes sense in the context of the sentence. Correlative conjunctions are pairs of conjunctions that work together within a sentence. An example of this would be in the sentence, "Not only is he very strong but he is also very smart".

Variation of sentence types

It is important to use different types of sentences. They add variety. A good writer uses simple sentences, compound sentences, and complex sentences. A simple sentence contains a subject and a verb. It is a complete thought. "Allen studies after school." A compound sentence has two independent ideas. The ideas are joined by a conjunction. Some conjunctions are *for, and, but* and *so.* "Ernest was busy playing soccer, so Ann took a swim by herself." A complex sentence is made up of an independent clause and at least one dependent clauses. "The movie that Joan saw was a comedy." A writer uses different types of sentences to make the writing more interesting to the reader.

Sentence fragments and run-on sentences

A sentence is a group of words that contains a complete thought. It has a subject and verb. A fragment is not a complete sentence. It is not a complete thought. "Ran through the field" is not a complete thought. It has a verb and a prepositional phrase. But it does not have a subject. A fragment can be missing either the subject or the verb. "The huge pine trees" is a fragment. It doesn't have a verb. A run-on sentence has two complete thoughts. They should be divided into two sentences. "My grandmother writes me it's fun hearing from her." This

- 14 -

is a run-on sentence. It needs to be broken up into two sentences. "My grandmother writes me. It's fun hearing from her."

<u>Example 1</u>
Identify the answer choice that is a sentence fragment:
A. Anita learned to swim.
B. Our class took a field trip to the zoo.
C. Rides his bike to soccer practice.
D. James went to the beach with his sister.

The correct answer is Choice C. This is a sentence fragment. It has a verb, "rides." It has a predicate "rides his bike to soccer practice." It tells what happened, but not who or what did it. It needs a subject. "He rides his bike to soccer practice" would be a complete sentence. Choices A, B, and D all have both a subject and a verb. In choice A, "Anita" is the subject and "learned" is the verb. In choice B, the subject is "class" and the verb is "took." In choice D "James" is the subject and "went" is the verb.

<u>Example 2</u>
Identify the answer choice that is a run-on sentence:
A. We built a fire and cooked hot dogs outside.
B. Lisa has a pet hamster which she loves to play with.
C. He plays soccer well and can run faster than his teammates.
D. Edgar is sitting in the restaurant he is waiting for his sister.

Choice D is the correct choice. It is a run-on sentence. It has two complete thoughts which should be separated by a period. "Edgar is sitting in the restaurant. He is waiting for his sister." Choice A has two thoughts but they are correctly joined by the conjunction *and*. Choice B has an independent and a dependent clause. The dependant clause starts with the word *which*. It is a complete sentence. Choice C also contains two thoughts, but they are joined by the conjunction *and* making it a complete sentence. Sometimes run-on sentences are separated by the semicolon. This is correct as well. "Edgar is sitting in the restaurant; he is waiting for his sister." This is correct, but the first word of the second complete thought is not capitalized in this case.

Complete sentences

A complete sentence has a subject and a verb. It expresses a complete thought or idea. For instance, this is a complete sentence: "Kim likes to swim." In this sentence "Kim" is the subject and "likes" is the noun. The predicate is "likes to swim." The sentence expresses a complete thought or idea. It tells the reader something about Kim. Some sentences are more complex than others. For instance read the following sentence. "Kim and Ann like to swim and to dance." In this sentence there is a compound subject: "Kim and Ann." The verb is "like" and the predicate is "like to swim and to dance." This sentence is more complex than the first sentence. It still expresses a complete thought or idea.

Subject-verb agreement

Identify the sentence in which the subject and verb agree:
A. The mothers is going to have to decide if he can go.
B. The orange juice taste very fresh.
C. One of the test questions were hard.
D. Everyone on the team has to sign up tomorrow.

In a sentence the subject and verb must agree. If the subject is plural, then the verb must be plural. If a subject is singular a verb must be singular. In choice A the subject is "mothers." This is a plural noun. The verb is "is going." This is a singular form of the verb. So this sentence is incorrect. In choice B the subject is "juice" and the verb is "taste." The subject is singular and the verb is plural, so they do not agree. In choice C the subject is "one," a singular noun, but the verb "were" is in a plural. The correct answer is choice D. "Everyone" is singular and so is "has."

Conventions of written language

The conventions of written language include capitalizing words correctly. Proper names are capitalized. The first word of a sentence is capitalized. Titles are capitalized. The names of countries are capitalized. The names of rivers are capitalized. The conventions also include using proper punctuation. This means using end marks correctly. End marks include periods, question marks, and exclamation marks. It means using commas correctly. It means using apostrophes correctly. Good penmanship is also important. Good penmanship helps a reader to understand what has been written. It means that the handwriting is neat and well formed. Using these conventions will help the author communicate clearly.

Quotation marks

Use quotation marks to enclose direct quotations of a person's words, spoken or written. Do not use quotation marks around indirect quotations. An indirect quotation reports someone's ideas without using that person's exact words. Set off long quotations of prose or poetry by indenting. Use single quotation marks to enclose a quotation within a quotation. Quotation marks should be used around the titles of short works: newspaper and magazine articles, poems, short stories, songs, episodes of television and radio programs, and subdivisions of books or web sites. Punctuation is used with quotation marks according to convention. Periods and commas are placed inside quotation marks, whereas colons and semicolons are placed outside quotation marks. Question marks and exclamation points are placed either inside or outside quotation marks, depending on the rest of the material in the sentence. Do not use quotation marks around the title of your own essay.

Commas

Identify which sentence which does not use commas correctly:
A. I think, David, that you received the highest grade on the test.
B. No, you do not have to do any English homework tonight.
C. Our plane landed in Miami Florida, after one stop in Atlanta.
D. He bought hotdogs, sodas, and chips at the fair.

Choice C does not use a comma correctly. There should be a comma after the city, *Miami* and before the state, *Florida*. Comma rules state that cities or towns are separated from states by commas. Choice A is correct. The name *David* is in a direct address so it should be separated from the rest of the sentence by commas. Choice B is correct also. The answer *No* should be set off from the rest of the sentence by a comma as well. Choice D is also correct since comma rules say that items in a series are to be separated by commas.

Apostrophes

Identify which sentence uses an apostrophe correctly:
A. Whos' playing tennis with Mandy this afternoon?
B. The actresses costumes' were made by her grandmother.
C. The three, adorable, newborn puppies are Mildred's.
D. Theyr'e going to the planetarium on Thursday with Jude.

Choice C is the correct answer. This sentence uses an apostrophe correctly. This apostrophe indicates possession. The puppies belong to Mildred. Choice A is incorrect. The apostrophe should be after the *o* not after *s*. Then it would indicate that the letter *i* was left out. *Who's* is a contraction for *who is*. Choice B is incorrect. The apostrophe should go after the word *actresses* not *costumes*. The costumes belong to the actress. Choice D is incorrect. The apostrophe is in the wrong spot. It should be before the *r* to show that this is contraction of *They are*.

End marks

All sentences must have an end mark, but each end mark indicates something different. A sentence may end with a period, a question mark, or an exclamation point. A period is used when the sentence is a statement. "Marcy has two brothers." This is a complete thought and it is a statement. When a sentence asks a question, a question mark is used. "How many brothers does Marcy have?" is a question. When reading such a sentence aloud, the question mark indicates to the reader to raise his or her voice. An exclamation point shows surprise, fear, excitement or joy. It indicates to the reader that the words should be read with strong feeling. "We won the game!"

Example 1
Identify mistakes in capitalization in the passage below:
> On january 12, which was a friday, We went to the museum of science on a
> Class trip. the class took a bus to the museum. It was a lot of fun. My teacher,
> mrs. Jones, and some parents came with us.

There are several errors in capitalization in the passage. The names of months should be capitalized, so "january" should be "January." The days of the week should be capitalized so "friday" should be "Friday." The next mistake is that "We" should not be capitalized. It is not the first word in a sentence. It is not a proper noun either. It should be "we." The names of museums should be capitalized, so "museum of science" should be "Museum of Science." There is no reason for "Class" to be capitalized, so that is incorrect and needs to be changed. The word "the" at the start of a sentence should be capitalized. A person's title should be capitalized so "mrs" should be "Mrs."

<u>Example 2</u>
Identify the capitalization and punctuation mistakes in the passage below:
> dear mrs. Kennedy,
> My Mother wants me to write to you and say that I am sorry that I broke
> Jimmys GI Joe doll. I am sorry. I did not mean to break it
> Sam

There are several capitalization and punctuation errors. The first word in a sentence should always be capitalized, so "dear" should be "Dear." A person's title and name should be capitalized, so it should be "Mrs. Kennedy" instead of "mrs. Kennedy." In the body of the letter, "Mother" is not a proper noun and does not have to be capitalized. The GI Joe doll belongs to Jimmy, so Jimmy should be in a possessive form, which means it needs an apostrophe and an "s": "Jimmy's." The last sentence does not end with a punctuation mark. It should have a period at the end.

Contractions

A contraction is a word formed by combining two other words. Contractions are often used to make writing flow more easily. When the words are formed, letters are left out. An apostrophe is used in place of the letters that were left out. For example, *can* and *not* combine to become can't. The apostrophe is put in place of the omitted letter. Some contractions are used often. Learning them is useful. *Aren't* is a combination of *are not*; *don't* is a combination of *do not*, *doesn't* is a combination of *does not* and *hasn't* is a combination of *has not*.

Possessives

Possessives show ownership. They often use apostrophes and the letter "s." For instance, a writer might say "The horse of Mary is gray," but this is awkward. Instead the correct way to show ownership is to use an apostrophe and the letter "s" to make the name "Mary" into a possessive. The writer would then say, "Mary's horse is gray." The apostrophe and "s" take the place of the "of" to show ownership or possession. The writer can check to see if a possessive is correct. The writer can do this by inserting the word "of" instead of using the apostrophe and "s" and see if the sentence makes sense.

Plural words

Most nouns follow a set of rules for plural words. Many nouns are made plural by adding an *s* to the end of the word. For example, *cat* would become *cats*, *dog* would become *dogs*, and so on. A noun ending in *y* usually drops the *y* and adds *ies*. Examples of this would be *baby* to *babies* and *pony* to *ponies*. However, if a word ends in a *vowel* and then a *y*, it is treated like a normal word, just adding an *s*. For example, *monkey* becomes *monkeys* and *boy* becomes *boys*. Nouns that end with *f* or *fe* replace the *f* with a *v* before adding *s* or *es*. Some examples of this rule are *shelf* to *shelves* and *knife* to *knives*. A noun that ends in *ch*, *sh*, *s*, *x*, or *z* becomes plural by adding *es* to the end of the word. *Fox* to *foxes*, *bus* to *buses*, and *bush* to *bushes* are examples of this rule. Most nouns that end in *o* just add an *s* to make them plural like *piano* to *pianos* or *video* to *videos*. Some nouns that end in a *consonant* and then *o* do follow a different rule. For these words, add *es* to make the plural form. Examples of these words are *volcano* to *volcanoes* and *potato* to *potatoes*.

<u>Irregular plurals</u>
There are some nouns that change a vowel sound when they become plural. These are a type of irregular plural. Some examples of these words are *goose* to *geese*, *man* to *men*, *mouse* to *mice*, *tooth* to *teeth*, and *woman* to *women*. *Woman* to *women* is doubly irregular because the vowel sound doesn't change in the syllable where the vowel changes, but it does change in the syllable where the vowel stays the same. There are other plural words that are irregular because they do not change form at all when going from singular to plural. These words include *moose*, *deer*, *fish*, and *sheep*.

Word structure

One way to figure out what a word means is to look at its parts. There are three possible parts of a word. The root is the main part of the word. In the word *unhappiness, happy* is the root or main part. The prefix is added to the front of the word to change the word's meaning. *Un-* is the prefix that was added. It means "not." The suffix is added to the end of the word. The suffix *-ness* means "the state of." So *unhappiness* means the state of not being happy. There are only a few common prefixes and suffixes. Learning them makes it easier to break words down to find the meaning.

<u>Example</u>
Identify the parts of the word *unmistakable* and figure out its meaning.
The root of *unmistakable* is *mistake.* The prefix is *un-.* The suffix is *-able. Mistake* can be either a noun or a verb. As a noun it means "an error or fault." As a verb it means "to understand wrongly." The prefix *un-* means *not.* The suffix *-able* means "capable of." By putting the parts together, the reader can figure out that *unmistakable* means "not capable of error or understanding wrongly." A synonym, or word that means the same thing, would be *obvious.* "Mrs. Smith's intentions were unmistakable." Note that when the root word ends in a vowel and the suffix begins with a vowel, the vowel at the end of the root word is sometimes dropped.

Practice Test #1

Practice Questions

Questions 1 – 7 pertain to the following passage:

Masters of the Seas

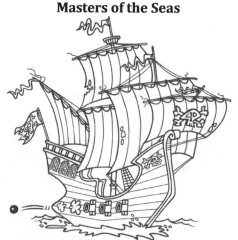

(1) Pirates have been sailing the seas for thousands of years. (2) The first recorded pirate raids occurred in 735 B.C. (3) During the middle ages, pirates lived mostly in Europe. (4) Later, pirates moved into the Caribbean, the South China Sea, and any other place with ships.

(5) Sometimes noblemen became pirates. (6) Some pirates were escaped slaves or criminals hiding from the law, others were gamblers, rebels, or people seeking adventure. (7) Even a few women were pirates!

(8) In spite of their different backgrounds; all pirates were looking for treasure. (9) They looked for real treasure such as gold, silver, and jewels. (10) They also looked for trading items such as spices, cloth, and tobacco. (11) In addition, pirates looked for useful items like tools, maps, and food.

(12) While many people think of pirates as part of history, there were still pirates on the seas today. (13) Modern pirates sail mostly near the coast of Africa, and they attack tanker ships and merchant ships. (14) Instead of treasure, today pirates ask for ransom money. (15) As long as there are ships sailing. (16) Pirates always will be around.

1. In sentence 3, what change, if any, should be made to the capitalization?

Ⓐ No change is necessary

Ⓑ Change middle ages to Middle ages

Ⓒ Change middle ages to Middle Ages

Ⓓ Change middle ages to middle Ages

- 20 -

2. Which sentence is the best choice for the first sentence of paragraph 2?

Ⓐ Sometimes noblemen became pirates

Ⓑ Although they all raided ships, pirates came from many different backgrounds

Ⓒ There were many ships on the seas, especially in the 1700s and 1800s

Ⓓ Pirates were very knowledgeable in geography, and they were all excellent sailors

3. What revision, if any, is needed in sentence 6?

Ⓐ No revision is necessary

Ⓑ Remove the comma between law and others

Ⓒ Change the comma between law and others to a semicolon followed by the word and

Ⓓ Change the comma between law and others to a period

4. Which change, if any, is needed in sentence 7?

Ⓐ No change is necessary

Ⓑ Change were to was

Ⓒ Change women to woman

Ⓓ Change few to several

5. Which of the following choices is the most correct version of sentence 8?

Ⓐ In spite of their different backgrounds; all pirates were looking for treasure

Ⓑ In spite of their different backgrounds, all pirates were looking for treasure

Ⓒ In spite of their different backgrounds. All pirates were looking for treasure

Ⓓ In spite of their different backgrounds; and all pirates were looking for treasure

6. Which change, if any, works best in sentence 12?

Ⓐ No change is necessary

Ⓑ Change were to was

Ⓒ Change were to are

Ⓓ Change were to is

- 21 -

7. Which revision, if any, is needed in sentences 15 and 16?

Ⓐ No revision is necessary

Ⓑ As long as there are ships sailing; pirates always will be around

Ⓒ As long as there are ships sailing. I think pirates always will be around

Ⓓ As long as there are ships sailing, pirates always will be around

Alicia wrote this report all about volcanoes. She would like your help revising her report. Read the report and look for places where Alicia could make revisions or improvements. When you are finished reading, answer the questions that follow.

Questions 8 – 14 pertain to the following passage:

The Power of Volcanoes

(1) The word *volcano* comes from *Vulcan*, the name of the ancient Roman god of fire. (2) A volcano occurs when hot, melted rock called magma breaks through the earth's crust. (3) I once saw a volcano erupt when I was on vacation in Hawaii. (4) When magma comes out on the surface of the earth and it is called lava. (5) Hot lava and ash often explode out of volcanoes, sometimes causing a lot of destruction.

(6) There are four basic types of volcanoes. (7) Shield volcanoes have broad, gentle slopes. (8) Cindercone volcanoes are pointed, kind of like pyramids. (9) Strato-volcanoes have many lairs of rock formed by hardened lava and ash from previous eruptions. (10) Dome volcanoes were shaped like steep mounds and are the result of slow-flowing lava.

(11) Whatever the type, volcanoes happen in places where the plates of the earth's crust touch each other. (12) There are many active volcanoes all over the world. (13) Some is in the United States, in places like Washington, Colorado, and Hawaii. (14) Some volcanoes are even under water, far below the surface of the ocean.

(15) When volcanoes erupt, they can change many things. (16) They can add height to mountains and even form new islands. (17) In Iceland, the island of Surtsey was formed by an erupting volcano in 1963. (18) Volcanoes can also collapse mountains. (19) At Crater Lake in Oregon, where a volcano collapsed a mountain, forming the deepest lake in the United States. (20) No matter their type or effects, everyone must agree that volcanoes are very powerful.

8. In sentence 1, what change, if any, should be made in capitalization?

Ⓐ No change is necessary

Ⓑ Change ancient Roman god to Ancient Roman God

Ⓒ Change ancient Roman god to ancient Roman God

Ⓓ Change ancient Roman god to ancient roman god

9. Which sentence does not belong in paragraph 1?

Ⓐ Sentence 1

Ⓑ Sentence 4

Ⓒ Sentence 3

Ⓓ Sentence 5

10. What revision, if any, is needed in sentence 4?

Ⓐ No revision is needed

Ⓑ Replace and with a comma

Ⓒ Insert a comma before and

Ⓓ Replace and with a semicolon

11. Which spelling change is needed in sentence 9?

Ⓐ Change volcanoes to volcanos

Ⓑ Change previous to pervious

Ⓒ Change eruptions to erupshuns

Ⓓ Change lairs to layers

12. What revision, if any, is necessary in sentence 10?

Ⓐ No revision is necessary

Ⓑ Change were to are

Ⓒ Change were to was

Ⓓ Change were to is

13. Which of the following is the best version of sentence 13?

Ⓐ Some is in the United States, in places like Washington, Colorado, and Hawaii

Ⓑ Some were in the United States, in places like Washington, Colorado, and Hawaii

Ⓒ Some was in the United States, in places like Washington, Colorado, and Hawaii

Ⓓ Some are in the United States, in places like Washington, Colorado, and Hawaii

14. Which change, if any, is needed in sentence 19?

Ⓐ No change is needed

Ⓑ Remove the comma after Oregon

Ⓒ Remove the word where

Ⓓ Replace the comma after Oregon with a semicolon

Questions 15 – 21 pertain to the following passage:

Down on the Farm

(1) On the day of the field trip, our classroom was buzzing with excitement. (2) Finally, the time came to get on the bus. (3) I watched out the window as big buildings slipped by, then houses and then fields. (4) The bus turned down a long, gravel driveway and stopped by a big red barn. (5) We were at the farm!

(6) We learned that Farmer Jones and his wife grew corn and pumpkins and raised cows and chickens. (7) First, we took a tour of the farm. (8) They had several farm workers to help take care of the farm. (9) Farmer Jones and his wife also have a small market where they sold there crops and some crops from other farmers who lived nearby.

(10) I loved walking through the cornfield with the dry stalks rustling above my head. (11) Farmer Jones also let me feed a calf from a bottle, and I loved feeling it suck and tug to get at the milk. (12) When we were done seeing the farm. (13) Farmer Jones took us all up to the market for some fresh, hot corn on the cob. (14) It was so yummy!

- 24 -

(15) When the time came to get back on the bus, no one wanted to leave. (16) We thanked Farmer Jones and headed back to town. (17) I loved visiting the farm and seeing how Farmer Jones lived maybe I will decide to be a farmer someday.

15. What spelling change, if any, is needed in sentence 1?

Ⓐ No change is needed

Ⓑ Change classroom to class room

Ⓒ Change buzzing to buzing

Ⓓ Change excitement to excitment

16. Which of the following choices is the best version of sentence 3?

Ⓐ I watched out the window as big buildings slipped by, then houses and then fields

Ⓑ I watched out the window as big buildings slipped by, then houses; and then fields

Ⓒ I watched out the window as big buildings slipped by, then houses, and then fields

Ⓓ I watched out the window as big buildings slipped by, then houses; then fields

17. Which sentence is the best choice for the first sentence of paragraph 2?

Ⓐ Sentence 6

Ⓑ Sentence 7

Ⓒ Sentence 8

Ⓓ Sentence 9

18. Which revision, if any, should be made to the verb *have* in sentence 9?

Ⓐ No revision is needed

Ⓑ Change have to had

Ⓒ Change have to has

Ⓓ Change have to having

19. Which of the following is the proper spelling choice for sentence 9?

Ⓐ They're

Ⓑ There

Ⓒ Thier

Ⓓ Their

20. What revision, if any, is needed in sentences 12 and 13?

Ⓐ No revision is needed

Ⓑ Change the period to a semicolon

Ⓒ Add Then at the beginning of sentence 13

Ⓓ Change the period to a comma

21. What change, if any, is necessary in sentence 17?

Ⓐ No change is necessary

Ⓑ Insert a comma after lived

Ⓒ Insert a period after lived

Ⓓ Insert a semicolon and and after lived

Questions 22 -28 pertain to the following passage:
Some People Never Learn

(1) One lazy Sunday afternoon, all the boys in our neighborhood decide to play football in the big field on the corner. (2) There used to be a gas station there, but a construction company knocked it down. (3) My brother, Seth, went to play, so I went along to watch. (4) It had rained all morning. (5) So the field was muddy and slick. (6) On the second play of the game, a big boy crashed into Seth and knocked him to the ground.

(7) I rushed over to Seth. (8) He was pale and shaking, and he was holding his arm. (9) He told me to run home and get Mom. (10) Mom came with the car, and we help Seth get in and buckle his seatbelt. (11) Then we did drive him to the hospital.

(12) In the emergency room, the doctors and nurses began working on Seth. (13) They sent him for x-rays and gave him some pills to make the pain better. (14) Then a doctor came in and said Seth broke his upper arm. (15) Seth's arm would have to be in a sling for six weeks to help it heal.

(16) For six long weeks, I helped Mom take care of Seth he needed help with almost everything. (17) Lucky for him, he didn't have to do chores for six weeks, and he even got to skip some of his schoolwork. (18) Finally Seth's arm was better, and he could take off the sling. (19) The very next day, Seth was back out in the field playing football. (20) Some people never learn!

22. What change, if any, is needed in sentence 1?

 Ⓐ No change is needed

 Ⓑ Change decide to decides

 Ⓒ Change decide to decided

 Ⓓ Change decide to deciding

23. Which sentence does not belong in this essay?

 Ⓐ Sentence 1

 Ⓑ Sentence 2

 Ⓒ Sentence 6

 Ⓓ Sentence 9

24. What revision, if any, is needed in sentences 4 and 5?

 Ⓐ No revision is needed

 Ⓑ Replace the period with a comma

 Ⓒ Replace the period with a semicolon

 Ⓓ Insert and at the beginning of sentence 5

25. Which change, if any, is needed in sentence 6?

 Ⓐ No change is needed

 Ⓑ Insert a comma after Seth

 Ⓒ Remove the comma after game

 Ⓓ Insert a semicolon after Seth

26. Which of the following is the most correct version of sentence 11?

 Ⓐ Then we did drive him to the hospital

 Ⓑ Then we drived him to the hospital

 Ⓒ Then we would drive him to the hospital

 Ⓓ Then we drove him to the hospital

27. What revision, if any, is necessary in sentence 16?

Ⓐ No revision is necessary

Ⓑ Insert a comma after Seth

Ⓒ Remove the comma after weeks

Ⓓ Insert a period after Seth

28. What change, if any, is needed in sentence 18?

Ⓐ No change is needed

Ⓑ Remove the comma after better

Ⓒ Insert a comma after Finally

Ⓓ Insert a semicolon after better

Writing Prompt

Write about the best gift you ever received.

Answers and Explanations

TEKS Standard §110.15(b)(21)(B)

1. C: The term *Middle Ages* refers to a specific period in history, and the name of a specific historical period always should be capitalized. Options A, B, and D all offer improper capitalization, making these choices incorrect.

TEKS Standard §110.15(b)(15)(C) and (18)(A)(i)

2. B: The topic sentence of a paragraph should introduce the main idea of the paragraph. Option B begins with a transition from paragraph 1 by mentioning that all pirates raid ships. It then introduces the topic of paragraph 2, which discusses the diverse background of pirates. Option A, the current topic sentence, discusses one possible background for pirates, but it does not represent fully the main idea of the paragraph. Options C and D are similar, both discussing an aspect of pirates, but these options do not introduce the overall main idea of paragraph 2.

TEKS Standard §110.15(b)(20)(C)

3. D: Sentence 6 is a type of run-on sentence called a comma splice. It contains two complete sentences joined only by a comma. The best option for correcting this sentence is to replace the comma with a period, creating two separate sentences. Options A and B retain the run-on structure of the sentence, making them incorrect options. Option C uses a semicolon to separate the independent clauses, but it unnecessarily adds the word *and* to the sentence, making it an incorrect option.

TEKS Standard §110.15(b)(20)

4. A: Sentence 7 is correct as it is written. Option B is incorrect because the subject of the sentence is plural, so a plural verb is necessary. Option C is incorrect because the sentence discusses more than one woman, making *women* the correct word choice. Option D is incorrect because changing *few* to *several* creates an awkward and improper sentence.

TEKS Standard §110.15(b)(20)(C) and (21)(C)(i)

5. B: The first part of sentence 8 is an introductory phrase, which is dependent, so it cannot stand on its own. A comma is the most appropriate punctuation to join an introductory phrase with its associated independent clause. Options A and D are not correct because a semicolon is not an appropriate punctuation choice for joining an introductory phrase with its associated independent clause. Option C is incorrect because the introductory phrase cannot be followed by a period, since it cannot stand on its own as a sentence.

TEKS Standard §110.15(b)(20)(A)(i)

6. C: Sentence 12 is written in present tense and has a plural subject, so the present tense, plural verb *are* is the best choice for this sentence. Option A is incorrect because it uses a past tense verb when the sentence is written in present tense. Option B is incorrect because it uses a past tense, singular verb when the sentence is written in present tense and the subject is plural. Option D is incorrect because it uses a singular verb when the subject of the sentence is plural.

TEKS Standard §110.15(b)(20)(B)
7. D: Sentence 15 is a sentence fragment. Careful reading shows that the best correction option connects the fragment of sentence 15 to sentence 16 with a comma, creating a single, strong sentence. Option A is incorrect because it retains sentence 15 as a fragment. Option B is incorrect because a semicolon cannot connect a dependent clause to an independent clause. Option C is incorrect because it only adds the words *I think*, retaining sentence 15 as a fragment.

TEKS Standard §110.15(b)(20)
8. A: The current capitalization is correct, since the only proper noun in the sentence is *Roman*. B is incorrect because it capitalizes *Ancient* and *God*, neither of which are proper nouns in this context. C is wrong because it capitalizes *God*, which is not a proper noun in this context. D is wrong it does not capitalize *roman*, which is a proper noun.

TEKS Standard §110.15(b)(15)(C)
9. C: Sentence 3 describes a personal experience that does not belong in a factual essay about volcanoes. A, B, and D are wrong because sentences 1, 4, and 5 all are essential to develop factual information about volcanoes.

TEKS Standard §110.15(b)(20) and (21)(C)
10. B: The sentence contains a dependent introductory clause, and a dependent introductory clause should always be separated from the main clause of the sentence with a comma. A and C are wrong because they both create a sentence fragment. C is incorrect because a semicolon cannot join a dependent clause to an independent clause.

TEKS Standard §110.15(b)(22)(C)
11. D: The misspelled word is *lairs*; it should be *layers*.

TEKS Standard §110.15(b)(20)(A)(i)
12. B: The subject of the sentence is plural and the essay is written in present tense, making *are* the right choice. A is wrong because *were* is a past-tense verb, and this passage is written in present tense. C incorrect because *was* is a singular, past-tense verb, and this sentence has a plural subject and is written in present tense. D is wrong because *is* is a singular verb, and the subject of this sentence is plural.

TEKS Standard §110.15(b)(20)(C)
13. D: This sentence has a plural subject, and this essay is written in present tense, so *are* is right choice. A is not correct because *is* is a singular verb, and the subject of this sentence is plural. B is wrong because *were* is a past-tense verb, and this essay is written in present tense. C is incorrect because *was* is a singular, past-tense verb, and this sentence has a plural subject and is written in present tense.

TEKS Standard §110.15(b)(20)
14. C: Removing *where* changes the sentence from a dependent clause to a complete sentence. A, B, and D are incorrect because they all retain the dependent clause, making the sentence a fragment—thus unable to stand on its own.

TEKS Standard §110.15(b)(22)
15. A: There are no misspelled words in the sentence, so no changes are necessary.

TEKS Standard §110.15(b)(21)(C)

16. C: is the correct answer because items in a series should always be separated by commas, including a comma just before the conjunction. A is wrong because it omits the comma before the conjunction. B and D are incorrect because they both improperly use a semicolon to separate items in a series when those items contain no internal commas.

TEKS Standard §110.15(b)(18)(A)(i)

17. B: Sentence 7 is the best choice because it clearly establishes the overall topic of the paragraph, which is what the first sentence of a paragraph should do. A, C, and D are all incorrect because they all offer details and specifics instead of establishing a broad overview of the paragraph.

TEKS Standard §110.15(b)(20)(A)(i)

18. B: This essay is written in past tense, so changing have to had makes this sentence match the rest of the story.

TEKS Standard §110.15(b)(22)(C)

19. D: *Their* is the proper spelling for a plural personal pronoun showing ownership. A is wrong because *they're* is a contraction of *they are*, which does not fit in the sentence. B is wrong because *there* refers to location. C is the right word, but it is misspelled.

TEKS Standard §110.15(b)(20)(B)

20. D: Sentence 12 is actually a dependent clause that should function as an introductory element to the independent clause in sentence 13, and an introductory dependent clause should be joined to the corresponding independent clause with a comma. A and C are incorrect because they leave sentence 12 as a sentence fragment. B is wrong because a semicolon should not join a dependent clause to an independent clause.

TEKS Standard §110.15(b)(20) and (21)

21. C: Adding a period eliminates the run-on sentence by creating two complete sentences. A is wrong because it retains the run-on sentence structure. B is incorrect because it creates a comma splice, another type of run-on sentence. D is wrong because a semicolon should not be used with a conjunction to join two independent clauses.

TEKS Standard §110.15(b)(20)(A)(i)

22. C: is correct because *decided* is a past-tense verb, and this passage is written in past tense. A is wrong because *decide* is a present-tense verb. B is incorrect because *decides* is a singular, present-tense verb, and this sentence has a plural subject and is written in past tense. D is wrong because *deciding* is a gerund form of the verb, which is not appropriate in this sentence.

TEKS Standard §110.15(b)(15) and (18)(A)(ii)

23. B: Sentence 2 gives unnecessary details. They don't help the reader understand the story any better, and are a distraction. A, C, and D are wrong because sentences 1, 6, and 9 all offer relevant information important to the development of the story.

TEKS Standard §110.15(b)(20)

24. B: Sentence 5 is a dependent clause that needs to be combined with sentence 4 through the use of a comma to form a complete sentence. A and D both retain sentence 5 as a sentence fragment. C is wrong because a semicolon should not join an independent clause to a dependent clause.

TEKS Standard §110.15(b)(20)

25. A: The sentence is correct as written.

TEKS Standard §110.15(b)(20)(A)(i)

26. D: The simple past-tense verb *drove* is appropriate for this story, since it is written in past tense.

TEKS Standard §110.15(b)(20) and (21)

27. D: Adding a period eliminates the run-on sentence and creates two complete sentences. A and C are wrong because they both retain the run-on sentence structure. B is incorrect because separating two independent clauses with only a comma creates a comma splice, which is also a type of run-on sentence.

TEKS Standard §110.15(b)(21)(C)

28. C: Because *Finally* is an introductory word in this sentence, it should be separated from the rest of the sentence with a comma.

Sample Written Piece for Writing Prompt:

The best gift I ever received was my puppy, Bear. It was a snowy Christmas morning, and all the presents had been opened. Then my parents brought out one more box. It was moving and whining. They gave it to me, and I opened it. It was Bear!

Ever since then, Bear has been my best friend. He sleeps in my bed with me. He loves to play with me and learn new tricks. Every day when I come home from school, Bear is waiting for me.

Bear will always be my best gift because he is always there for me. I can tell him anything. Even though he is getting bigger, he still loves me, just like he did when he was a little puppy. I am so glad Bear is mine.

Practice Test #2

Practice Questions

Questions 1 – 7 pertain to the following passage:

Clara Barton: A Heart for Helping

(1) Clara barton was born on Christmas in 1821. (2) She lived in North Oxford, Massachusetts, and was the youngest of five children. (3) Although she loved sports, reading, and horseback riding, Clara mostly enjoyed helping people. (4) In fact, when she was only 11. (5) Clara spent two years caring for her brother after he suffered a serious injury.

(6) Clara becomes a teacher while she was still a teenager because she loved to help so much. (7) After teaching for many years, Clara moved to Washington D.C. to work in the Patent Office, where she gave permits to new inventors. (8) In 1861, the Civil War began, and Clara used her free time to gather supplies for soldiers.

(9) In 1862, Clara started traveling to battlefields to help wounded soldiers and deliver food and supplies. (10) Even though she was not a nurse, Clara saved the lives of many soldiers. (11) The Civil War was fought over many issues, including slavery. (12) When the war ended, she continued to give speeches to people about the bad conditions on battlefields. (13) Many people heard Clara speak.

(14) In 1869, Clara traveled to Switzerland to visit some friends. (15) While there, she learned about a new organization called the International Red Cross, Clara began working with them. (16) In 1881, she returned to the United States and established the American Red Cross. (17) Then Clara spends the rest of her life doing what she loved best: helping people.

1. Which version of sentence 1 is capitalized correctly?

Ⓐ Clara barton was born on Christmas in 1821

Ⓑ Clara Barton was born on Christmas in 1821

Ⓒ Clara Barton was born on christmas in 1821

Ⓓ Clara barton was born on christmas in 1821

2. What revision, if any, is needed in sentence 4?

Ⓐ No revision is needed

Ⓑ Remove the period

Ⓒ Replace the period with a semicolon

Ⓓ Replace the period with a comma

3. What change, if any, is necessary in sentence 6?

Ⓐ No change is necessary

Ⓑ Change loved to loves

Ⓒ Change becomes to became

Ⓓ Change was to were

4. What spelling correction, if any, is needed in sentence 9?

Ⓐ No correction is needed

Ⓑ Change traveling to travelling

Ⓒ Change battlefields to battlefeilds

Ⓓ Change soldiers to souldiers

5. Which sentence does not belong in this essay?

Ⓐ Sentence 4

Ⓑ Sentence 7

Ⓒ Sentence 11

Ⓓ Sentence 15

6. What revision, if any, is needed in sentence 15?

Ⓐ No revision is needed

Ⓑ Replace the comma after Cross with a period

Ⓒ Remove the comma after Cross

Ⓓ Replace the comma after there with a semicolon

7. What change, if any, is necessary in sentence 17?

Ⓐ No change is necessary

Ⓑ Replace helping with helped

Ⓒ Replace loved with loves

Ⓓ Replace spends with spent

Questions 8 – 14 pertain to the following passages:
Amazing Pandas

(1) When a baby panda is born, it is about the size of a breakfast sausage. (2) Tiny and almost furless, it snuggled close to its mother. (3) The baby panda stays very near its mother for the first two months of life. (4) Because until it is two months old, the panda's eyes cannot open. (5) It relies on its mother for everything.

(6) Even when the baby panda's eyes are open, it still needs its mother for food. (7) Baby pandas nurse from their mothers up to eight times a day until they are 18 months old. (8) During this time they also chew on bamboo but this is just for fun. (9) Their teeth are not strong enough to really eat the bamboo.

(10) Bamboo does not have many vitamins and calories, though, so pandas must spend up to 14 hours a day eating just to stay full! (11) Sometime between 12 and 18 months of age, pandas begin really eating bamboo. (12) Even so, they do not wander far from home; pandas stay with their mothers until they are full grown.
(13) When a full grown panda is about five feet long and weighs about 200 pounds. (14) They live in the forests of China, although many now live in zoos and other places. (15) In fact, there were only about 1600 pandas left in the wild, because their habitats have been destroyed to build cities. (16) People need to care for pandas so these amazing animals will always be with us.

8. What change, if any, is needed in sentence 2?

Ⓐ No change is needed

Ⓑ Change furless to fur-less

Ⓒ Change snuggled to snuggles

Ⓓ Change its to it's

9. What revision, if any, is necessary in sentence 3?

Ⓐ No revision is necessary

Ⓑ Replace the period with a comma

Ⓒ Replace the period with a semicolon

Ⓓ Remove the period

10. What change, if any, is needed in sentence 8?

Ⓐ No change is needed

Ⓑ Insert a period after bamboo

Ⓒ Insert a comma after bamboo

Ⓓ Insert a semicolon after bamboo

11. Which sentence is the best choice for the first sentence of paragraph 3?

Ⓐ Sentence 10

Ⓑ Sentence 12

Ⓒ Sentence 9

Ⓓ Sentence 11

12. What revision, if any, is necessary in sentence 12?

Ⓐ No revision is necessary

Ⓑ Replace the semicolon with a comma

Ⓒ Remove the comma after so

Ⓓ Change the period to an exclamation point

13. What change, if any, is needed in sentence 13?

Ⓐ No change is needed

Ⓑ Remove the period to combine sentence 13 with sentence 14

Ⓒ Insert a comma after long

Ⓓ Remove the word When

14. What revision, if any, is necessary in sentence 15?

Ⓐ No revision is necessary

Ⓑ Change were to are

Ⓒ Change 1600 to sixteen hundred

Ⓓ Change their to there

Questions 15 – 21 pertain to the following passage:

Niagara Falls

(1) Last Summer, my family went on a trip to Niagara Falls in New York. (2) Niagara Falls is a famous waterfall that flows between the United States and Canada. (3) When I first saw the falls. (4) I couldn't believe it. (5) It was huge! (6) I had never seen so much water in my life.

(7) To get a better look at the falls, we decided to take a boat ride to the base of the falls, where the waterfall crashes into the river. (8) We got on a boat with a lot of other people. (9) Every person was given a blue plastic rain poncho. (10) As we got closer to the bottom of the falls, I knew why. (11) The water sprayed up like it was raining, and the crashing is so loud I couldn't even hear myself yell.

(12) We saw another boat, far below us, headed for the base of Niagara Falls. (13) When the boat ride was over, we drove back to the top of the falls and walked along the sidewalk. (14) The falls was so big it made the boat look like a toy and the people look like tiny insects.

(15) Before we left Niagara Falls, I bought some postcards at a gift shop. (16) When we got home, I used the post cards to make a new page for my scrapbook. (17) I also wrote down some of my memories from the trip. (18) Then I will always remember my trip to Niagara Falls.

15. Which of the following versions of sentence 1 contains proper capitalization?

Ⓐ Last Summer, my family went on a trip to Niagara Falls in New York

Ⓑ Last summer, my family went on a trip to niagara falls in New York

Ⓒ Last summer, my family went on a trip to Niagara Falls in New York

Ⓓ Last Summer, my family went on a trip to Niagara Falls in new york

16. What revision, if any, is necessary in sentences 3 and 4?

Ⓐ No revision is necessary

Ⓑ Replace the period with a comma

Ⓒ Remove the period

Ⓓ Replace the period with and

17. What change, if any, is needed in sentence 11?

Ⓐ No change is needed

Ⓑ Change sprayed to sprays

Ⓒ Change was to is

Ⓓ Change is to was

18. Which sentence is the best choice as the first sentence of paragraph 3?

Ⓐ Sentence 12

Ⓑ Sentence 13

Ⓒ Sentence 11

Ⓓ Sentence 14

19. Which revision, if any, is necessary in sentence 14?

Ⓐ No revision is necessary

Ⓑ Insert a comma after big

Ⓒ Insert a semicolon after toy

Ⓓ Insert a comma after tiny

20. Which of the following reflects the correct spelling?

Ⓐ Niagra Falls

Ⓑ Nyagra Falls

Ⓒ Niagara Falls

Ⓓ Niagira Falls

21. What change, if any, is needed in sentence 18?

Ⓐ No change is needed

Ⓑ Change remember to remembered

Ⓒ Change will to would

Ⓓ Change Then to Now

Questions 22 – 28 pertain to the following passage:
A Night to Be Remembered

(1) At the beginning of the year, my teacher announced that our school was going to have a speech contest. (2) It sounded like fun. (3) So I decided to enter. (4) I thought and thought about what to say in my speech. (5) Then I go to the library and did some research.

(6) I decided to write my speech about the life and accomplishments of Dr. Martin Luther King Jr. (7) He is one of my favorite people, and I wrote the best speech ever. (8) When I was done, I read the speech to my parents. (9) My dad once gave a speech to the city council. (10) They loved it!

(11) On the night of the speech contest, I was very nervous. (12) My stomach was flip-flopping even through I knew my speech by heart. (13) When it was my turn, I took a deep breath, stood up, and gave my speech perfectly. (14) Everyone clapped, and I sat down. (15) Then I had to wait for the judges' decision.

(16) After what seemed like forever, the head judge stood up and said it was a close concert and everyone did well. (17) Then he announced that I won first place! (18) I was so surprised that my head was spinning and my knees were wobbly. (19) After everyone cheered, and my parents took me out for ice cream. (20) It was a night I will never forget.

22. What revision, if any, is needed in sentences 2 and 3?

Ⓐ No revision is needed

Ⓑ Replace the period with a comma

Ⓒ Remove the period

Ⓓ Insert And at the beginning of sentence 3

23. What change, if any, is necessary in sentence 5?

(A) No change is necessary

(B) Change go to did go

(C) Change go to went

(D) Change did to done

24. Which version of sentence 6 reflects correct capitalization?

(A) I decided to write my speech about the life and accomplishments of Dr. Martin Luther King Jr.

(B) I decided to write my speech about the life and accomplishments of dr. Martin Luther King Jr.

(C) I decided to write my speech about the life and accomplishments of Dr. Martin luther King jr.

(D) I decided to write my speech about the life and accomplishments of Dr. Martin Luther King jr.

25. Which sentence does not belong in this story?

(A) Sentence 2

(B) Sentence 7

(C) Sentence 9

(D) Sentence 15

26. What spelling correction, if any, is needed in sentence 12?

(A) No correction is needed

(B) Change stomach to stomache

(C) Change flip-flopping to flipflopping

(D) Change through to though

27. Which revision, if any, is necessary in the wording of sentence 16?

(A) No revision is necessary

(B) Change head to heard

(C) Change well to good

(D) Change concert to contest

28. What change, if any, is needed in sentence 19?

Ⓐ No change is needed

Ⓑ Remove the word After

Ⓒ Remove the comma after cheered

Ⓓ Replace the comma after cheered with a semicolon

Writing Prompt

Write about your favorite vacation.

Answers and Explanations

TEKS Standard §110.15(b)(21)(B)

1. B: *Clara Barton* and *Christmas* both are proper nouns and should be capitalized.

TEKS Standard §110.15(b)(20) and (21)(C)

2. D: Sentence 4 is actually a sentence fragment, not a complete sentence. It is an introductory, dependent clause for sentence 5, and an introductory clause links to the corresponding independent clause with a comma

TEKS Standard §110.15(b)(20)(A)(i)

3. C: This passage is written in past tense and *became* is the past-tense verb form

TEKS Standard §110.15(b)(22)

4. A: All words in the sentence currently are spelled correctly, so no change is necessary.

TEKS Standard §110.15(b)(15) and (18)(A)(ii)

5. C: Sentence 11 offers a fact that has nothing to do with an essay about Clara Barton, so it doesn't belong in this passage. Sentences 4, 7, and 15 all are necessary for the development of this essay.

TEKS Standard §110.15(b)(20) and (21)(C)

6. B: Replacing the comma after *Cross* with a period eliminates the run-on sentence by creating two separate, complete sentences.

TEKS Standard §110.15(b)(20)(A)(i)

7. D: The present-tense verb *spends* should be replaced with the past-tense verb *spent*, because this passage is written in past tense.

TEKS Standard §110.15(b)(20)(A)(i)

8. C: The word *snuggled* is a past-tense verb and this passage is written in present tense, so it should be changed to *snuggles* to match the rest of the passage.

TEKS Standard §110.15(b)(20) and (21)(C)(i)

9. B: Sentence 4 is a dependent clause that should link to the independent clause in sentence 3 with a comma to create a complete sentence.

TEKS Standard §110.15(b)(20) and (21)(C)(i)

10. C: A comma should be used just before a coordinating conjunction that connects two independent clauses.

TEKS Standard §110.15(b)(18)(A)(i)

11. D: Sentence 11 gives broad information about the topic of the paragraph, making it the best choice as the first sentence of the paragraph. Also, in its current form, the sentences are out of order, so sentence 10 doesn't make much sense. It does make sense if sentence 11 is put in front of it.

TEKS Standard §110.15(b)(20)
12. A: Sentence 12 is correct as written, so no change is necessary.

TEKS Standard §110.15(b)(15) and (20)
13. D: Removing *When* allows the sentence to stand on its own as a proper sentence.

TEKS Standard §110.15(b)(20)(A)(i)
14. B: The word *were* is a past-tense verb, and this passage is written in present tense, so it should be changed to *are*.

TEKS Standard §110.15(b)(20)(B)
15. C: The word *summer* is not a proper noun and should not be capitalized, but *Niagara Falls* and *New York* are proper nouns and do require capitalization.

TEKS Standard §110.15(b)(20)
16. B: Sentence 3 is an introductory, dependent clause that needs to be joined with a comma to the independent clause in sentence 4.

TEKS Standard §110.15(b)(20)(A)(i)
17. D: The word *is* should be changed to *was*, because *was* is a past-tense verb, and this passage is written in past tense.

TEKS Standard §110.15(b)(18)(A)(i)
18. B: Sentence 12 is out of order; it should come after sentence 13. Sentence 13, which introduces the broad, overall topic of the paragraph, should come first.

TEKS Standard §110.15(b)(20)
19. A: Sentence 14 is correct as written; no change is needed.

TEKS Standard §110.15(b)(22)
20. C: This is the correct spelling of *Niagara Falls*.

TEKS Standard §110.15(b)(20)
21. D: This is the correct answer because *Now* is in present tense and fits the tone and present tense of the sentence.

TEKS Standard §110.15(b)(20)
22. B: Sentence 3 is a dependent clause that should be joined to the independent clause in sentence 2 with a comma.

TEKS Standard §110.15(b)(20)(A)(i)
23. C: Changing *go* to *went* is correct because *went* is a past-tense verb, and this passage is written in past tense. *Go* is a present tense verb and does not match the rest of the passage.

TEKS Standard §110.15(b)(21)(B)
24. A: is the best choice because it contains the most appropriate capitalization. All the words in *Dr. Martin Luther King, Jr.* should be capitalized.

TEKS Standard §110.15(b)(15)(C)

25. C: Sentence 9 contains information irrelevant to the story. The fact that the author's dad once gave a speech in front of city council is interesting, but it has nothing to do with the story being told in this passage. If the author wants to talk about that, he should write another story and mention it in that piece, not this one.

TEKS Standard §110.15(b)(22)
26. D: is correct; *though* is the most appropriate word for this sentence.

TEKS Standard §110.15(b)(15)(D)
27. D: The word *contest* is the best word choice for this sentence; the author is confusing the meaning of *concert* with *contest*.

TEKS Standard §110.15(b)(20)
28. B: Removing the word *After* allows the sentence to stand on its own as a complete sentence.

Sample Written Piece for Writing Prompt:

My favorite vacation ever was when my family went to Jamaica last summer. We rode on an airplane and landed in Jamaica in the afternoon. The weather was sunny and very hot, but our hotel was nice and cool.

On our second day in Jamaica, we went to Dunn's River Falls. It is an awesome waterfall, and you can climb up to the top. We also visited a craft market where people sold necklaces and coasters and things they had carved out of wood and bamboo. Back at the hotel, some of our best times were spent swimming in the huge pool.

When the time came to leave Jamaica, I was very sad to go. I knew I would miss all the fun times I had there. I will always remember my family trip to Jamaica. It was the best vacation I ever had.

Success Strategies

The most important thing you can do is to ignore your fears and jump into the test immediately- do not be overwhelmed by any strange-sounding terms. You have to jump into the test like jumping into a pool- all at once is the easiest way.

Make Predictions

As you read and understand the question, try to guess what the answer will be. Remember that several of the answer choices are wrong, and once you begin reading them, your mind will immediately become cluttered with answer choices designed to throw you off. Your mind is typically the most focused immediately after you have read the question and digested its contents. If you can, try to predict what the correct answer will be. You may be surprised at what you can predict.

Quickly scan the choices and see if your prediction is in the listed answer choices. If it is, then you can be quite confident that you have the right answer. It still won't hurt to check the other answer choices, but most of the time, you've got it!

Answer the Question

It may seem obvious to only pick answer choices that answer the question, but the test writers can create some excellent answer choices that are wrong. Don't pick an answer just because it sounds right, or you believe it to be true. It MUST answer the question. Once you've made your selection, always go back and check it against the question and make sure that you didn't misread the question, and the answer choice does answer the question posed.

Benchmark

After you read the first answer choice, decide if you think it sounds correct or not. If it doesn't, move on to the next answer choice. If it does, mentally mark that answer choice. This doesn't mean that you've definitely selected it as your answer choice, it just means that it's the best you've seen thus far. Go ahead and read the next choice. If the next choice is worse than the one you've already selected, keep going to the next answer choice. If the next choice is better than the choice you've already selected, mentally mark the new answer choice as your best guess.

The first answer choice that you select becomes your standard. Every other answer choice must be benchmarked against that standard. That choice is correct until proven otherwise by another answer choice beating it out. Once you've decided that no other answer choice seems as good, do one final check to ensure that your answer choice answers the question posed.

Valid Information

Don't discount any of the information provided in the question. Every piece of information may be necessary to determine the correct answer. None of the information in the question is there to throw you off (while the answer choices will certainly have information to throw you off). If two seemingly unrelated topics are discussed, don't ignore either. You can be confident there is a relationship, or it wouldn't be included in the question, and you are probably going to have to determine what is that relationship to find the answer.

Avoid "Fact Traps"

Don't get distracted by a choice that is factually true. Your search is for the answer that answers the question. Stay focused and don't fall for an answer that is true but incorrect. Always go back to the question and make sure you're choosing an answer that actually answers the question and is not just a true statement. An answer can be factually correct, but it MUST answer the question asked. Additionally, two answers can both be seemingly correct, so be sure to read all of the answer choices, and make sure that you get the one that BEST answers the question.

Milk the Question

Some of the questions may throw you completely off. They might deal with a subject you have not been exposed to, or one that you haven't reviewed in years. While your lack of knowledge about the subject will be a hindrance, the question itself can give you many clues that will help you find the correct answer. Read the question carefully and look for clues. Watch particularly for adjectives and nouns describing difficult terms or words that you don't recognize. Regardless of if you completely understand a word or not, replacing it with a synonym either provided or one you more familiar with may help you to understand what the questions are asking. Rather than wracking your mind about specific detailed information concerning a difficult term or word, try to use mental substitutes that are easier to understand.

The Trap of Familiarity

Don't just choose a word because you recognize it. On difficult questions, you may not recognize a number of words in the answer choices. The test writers don't put "make-believe" words on the test; so don't think that just because you only recognize all the words in one answer choice means that answer choice must be correct. If you only recognize words in one answer choice, then focus on that one. Is it correct? Try your best to determine if it is correct. If it is, that is great, but if it doesn't, eliminate it. Each word and answer choice you eliminate increases your chances of getting the question correct, even if you then have to guess among the unfamiliar choices.

Eliminate Answers

Eliminate choices as soon as you realize they are wrong. But be careful! Make sure you consider all of the possible answer choices. Just because one appears right, doesn't mean that the next one won't be even better! The test writers will usually put more than one good answer choice for every question, so read all of them. Don't worry if you are stuck between two that seem right. By getting down to just two remaining possible choices, your odds are now 50/50. Rather than wasting too much time, play the odds. You are guessing, but guessing wisely, because you've been able to knock out some of the answer choices that you know are wrong. If you are eliminating choices and realize that the last answer choice you are left with is also obviously wrong, don't panic. Start over and consider each choice again. There may easily be something that you missed the first time and will realize on the second pass.

Tough Questions

If you are stumped on a problem or it appears too hard or too difficult, don't waste time. Move on! Remember though, if you can quickly check for obviously incorrect answer choices, your chances of guessing correctly are greatly improved. Before you completely give up, at least try to knock out a couple of possible answers. Eliminate what you can and then guess at the remaining answer choices before moving on.

Brainstorm

If you get stuck on a difficult question, spend a few seconds quickly brainstorming. Run through the complete list of possible answer choices. Look at each choice and ask yourself, "Could this answer the question satisfactorily?" Go through each answer choice and consider it independently of the other. By systematically going through all possibilities, you may find something that you would otherwise overlook. Remember that when you get stuck, it's important to try to keep moving.

Read Carefully

Understand the problem. Read the question and answer choices carefully. Don't miss the question because you misread the terms. You have plenty of time to read each question thoroughly and make sure you understand what is being asked. Yet a happy medium must be attained, so don't waste too much time. You must read carefully, but efficiently.

Face Value

When in doubt, use common sense. Always accept the situation in the problem at face value. Don't read too much into it. These problems will not require you to make huge leaps of logic. The test writers aren't trying to throw you off with a cheap trick. If you have to go beyond creativity and make a leap of logic in order to have an answer choice answer the question, then you should look at the other answer choices. Don't overcomplicate the problem by creating theoretical relationships or explanations that will warp time or space. These are normal problems rooted in reality. It's just that the applicable relationship or explanation may not be readily apparent and you have to figure things out. Use your common sense to interpret anything that isn't clear.

Prefixes

If you're having trouble with a word in the question or answer choices, try dissecting it. Take advantage of every clue that the word might include. Prefixes and suffixes can be a huge help. Usually they allow you to determine a basic meaning. Pre- means before, post- means after, pro - is positive, de- is negative. From these prefixes and suffixes, you can get an idea of the general meaning of the word and try to put it into context. Beware though of any traps. Just because con is the opposite of pro, doesn't necessarily mean congress is the opposite of progress!

Hedge Phrases

Watch out for critical "hedge" phrases, such as likely, may, can, will often, sometimes, often, almost, mostly, usually, generally, rarely, sometimes. Question writers insert these hedge phrases to cover every possibility. Often an answer choice will be wrong simply because it leaves no room for exception. Avoid answer choices that have definitive words like "exactly," and "always".

Switchback Words

Stay alert for "switchbacks". These are the words and phrases frequently used to alert you to shifts in thought. The most common switchback word is "but". Others include although, however, nevertheless, on the other hand, even though, while, in spite of, despite, regardless of.

New Information

Correct answer choices will rarely have completely new information included. Answer choices typically are straightforward reflections of the material asked about and will directly relate to the question. If a new piece of information is included in an answer choice that doesn't even seem to relate to the topic being asked about, then that answer choice is likely incorrect. All of the information needed to answer the question is usually provided for you, and so you should not have to make guesses that are unsupported or choose answer choices that require unknown information that cannot be reasoned on its own.

Time Management

On technical questions, don't get lost on the technical terms. Don't spend too much time on any one question. If you don't know what a term means, then since you don't have a dictionary, odds are you aren't going to get much further. You should immediately recognize terms as whether or not you know them. If you don't, work with the other clues that you have, the other answer choices and terms provided, but don't waste too much time trying to figure out a difficult term.

Contextual Clues

Look for contextual clues. An answer can be right but not correct. The contextual clues will help you find the answer that is most right and is correct. Understand the context in which a phrase or statement is made. This will help you make important distinctions.

Don't Panic

Panicking will not answer any questions for you. Therefore, it isn't helpful. When you first see the question, if your mind goes blank, take a deep breath. Force yourself to mechanically go through the steps of solving the problem and using the strategies you've learned.

Pace Yourself

Don't get clock fever. It's easy to be overwhelmed when you're looking at a page full of questions, your mind is full of random thoughts and feeling confused, and the clock is ticking down faster than you would like. Calm down and maintain the pace that you have set for yourself. As long as you are on track by monitoring your pace, you are guaranteed to have enough time for yourself. When you get to the last few minutes of the test, it may seem like you won't have enough time left, but if you only have as many questions as you should have left at that point, then you're right on track!

Answer Selection

The best way to pick an answer choice is to eliminate all of those that are wrong, until only one is left and confirm that is the correct answer. Sometimes though, an answer choice may immediately look right. Be careful! Take a second to make sure that the other choices are not equally obvious. Don't make a hasty mistake. There are only two times that you should stop before checking other answers. First is when you are positive that the answer choice you have selected is correct. Second is when time is almost out and you have to make a quick guess!

Check Your Work

Since you will probably not know every term listed and the answer to every question, it is important that you get credit for the ones that you do know. Don't miss any questions through careless mistakes. If at all possible, try to take a second to look back over your answer selection and make sure you've selected the correct answer choice and haven't made a costly careless mistake (such as marking an answer choice that you didn't mean to mark). This quick double check should more than pay for itself in caught mistakes for the time it costs.

Beware of Directly Quoted Answers

Sometimes an answer choice will repeat word for word a portion of the question or reference section. However, beware of such exact duplication – it may be a trap! More than likely, the correct choice will paraphrase or summarize a point, rather than being exactly the same wording.

Slang

Scientific sounding answers are better than slang ones. An answer choice that begins "To compare the outcomes…" is much more likely to be correct than one that begins "Because some people insisted…"

Extreme Statements

Avoid wild answers that throw out highly controversial ideas that are proclaimed as established fact. An answer choice that states the "process should be used in certain situations, if…" is much more likely to be correct than one that states the "process should be discontinued completely." The first is a calm rational statement and doesn't even make a definitive, uncompromising stance, using a hedge word "if" to provide wiggle room, whereas the second choice is a radical idea and far more extreme.

Answer Choice Families

When you have two or more answer choices that are direct opposites or parallels, one of them is usually the correct answer. For instance, if one answer choice states "x increases" and another answer choice states "x decreases" or "y increases," then those two or three answer choices are very similar in construction and fall into the same family of answer choices. A family of answer choices is when two or three answer choices are very similar in construction, and yet often have a directly opposite meaning. Usually the correct answer choice will be in that family of answer choices. The "odd man out" or answer choice that doesn't seem to fit the parallel construction of the other answer choices is more likely to be incorrect.

How to Overcome Test Anxiety

The very nature of tests caters to some level of anxiety, nervousness or tension, just as we feel for any important event that occurs in our lives. A little bit of anxiety or nervousness can be a good thing. It helps us with motivation, and makes achievement just that much sweeter. However, too much anxiety can be a problem; especially if it hinders our ability to function and perform.

"Test anxiety," is the term that refers to the emotional reactions that some test-takers experience when faced with a test or exam. Having a fear of testing and exams is based upon a rational fear, since the test-taker's performance can shape the course of an academic career. Nevertheless, experiencing excessive fear of examinations will only interfere with the test-takers ability to perform, and his/her chances to be successful.

There are a large variety of causes that can contribute to the development and sensation of test anxiety. These include, but are not limited to lack of performance and worrying about issues surrounding the test.

Lack of Preparation

Lack of preparation can be identified by the following behaviors or situations:

Not scheduling enough time to study, and therefore cramming the night before the test or exam
Managing time poorly, to create the sensation that there is not enough time to do everything
Failing to organize the text information in advance, so that the study material consists of the entire text and not simply the pertinent information
Poor overall studying habits

Worrying, on the other hand, can be related to both the test taker, or many other factors around him/her that will be affected by the results of the test. These include worrying about:

Previous performances on similar exams, or exams in general
How friends and other students are achieving
The negative consequences that will result from a poor grade or failure

There are three primary elements to test anxiety. Physical components, which involve the same typical bodily reactions as those to acute anxiety (to be discussed below). Emotional factors have to do with fear or panic. Mental or cognitive issues concerning attention spans and memory abilities.

Physical Signals

There are many different symptoms of test anxiety, and these are not limited to mental and emotional strain. Frequently there are a range of physical signals that will let a test taker know that he/she is suffering from test anxiety. These bodily changes can include the following:

Perspiring
Sweaty palms
Wet, trembling hands
Nausea
Dry mouth
A knot in the stomach
Headache
Faintness
Muscle tension
Aching shoulders, back and neck
Rapid heart beat
Feeling too hot/cold

To recognize the sensation of test anxiety, a test-taker should monitor him/herself for the following sensations:

The physical distress symptoms as listed above
Emotional sensitivity, expressing emotional feelings such as the need to cry or laugh too much, or a sensation of anger or helplessness
A decreased ability to think, causing the test-taker to blank out or have racing thoughts that are hard to organize or control.

Though most students will feel some level of anxiety when faced with a test or exam, the majority can cope with that anxiety and maintain it at a manageable level. However, those who cannot are faced with a very real and very serious condition, which can and should be controlled for the immeasurable benefit of this sufferer.

Naturally, these sensations lead to negative results for the testing experience. The most common effects of test anxiety have to do with nervousness and mental blocking.

Nervousness

Nervousness can appear in several different levels:

The test-taker's difficulty, or even inability to read and understand the questions on the test
The difficulty or inability to organize thoughts to a coherent form
The difficulty or inability to recall key words and concepts relating to the testing questions (especially essays)

The receipt of poor grades on a test, though the test material was well known by the test taker

Conversely, a person may also experience mental blocking, which involves:

Blanking out on test questions
Only remembering the correct answers to the questions when the test has already finished.

Fortunately for test anxiety sufferers, beating these feelings, to a large degree, has to do with proper preparation. When a test taker has a feeling of preparedness, then anxiety will be dramatically lessened.

The first step to resolving anxiety issues is to distinguish which of the two types of anxiety are being suffered. If the anxiety is a direct result of a lack of preparation, this should be considered a normal reaction, and the anxiety level (as opposed to the test results) shouldn't be anything to worry about. However, if, when adequately prepared, the test-taker still panics, blanks out, or seems to overreact, this is not a fully rational reaction. While this can be considered normal too, there are many ways to combat and overcome these effects.

Remember that anxiety cannot be entirely eliminated, however, there are ways to minimize it, to make the anxiety easier to manage. Preparation is one of the best ways to minimize test anxiety. Therefore the following techniques are wise in order to best fight off any anxiety that may want to build.

To begin with, try to avoid cramming before a test, whenever it is possible. By trying to memorize an entire term's worth of information in one day, you'll be shocking your system, and not giving yourself a very good chance to absorb the information. This is an easy path to anxiety, so for those who suffer from test anxiety, cramming should not even be considered an option.

Instead of cramming, work throughout the semester to combine all of the material which is presented throughout the semester, and work on it gradually as the course goes by, making sure to master the main concepts first, leaving minor details for a week or so before the test.

To study for the upcoming exam, be sure to pose questions that may be on the examination, to gauge the ability to answer them by integrating the ideas from your texts, notes and lectures, as well as any supplementary readings.

If it is truly impossible to cover all of the information that was covered in that particular term, concentrate on the most important portions, that can be covered very well. Learn these concepts as best as possible, so that when the test comes, a goal can be made to use these concepts as presentations of your knowledge.

In addition to study habits, changes in attitude are critical to beating a struggle with test anxiety. In fact, an improvement of the perspective over the entire test-taking experience can actually help a test taker to enjoy studying and therefore improve the overall experience. Be certain not to overemphasize the significance of the grade - know that the result of the test is neither a reflection of self worth, nor is it a measure of intelligence; one grade will not predict a person's future success.

To improve an overall testing outlook, the following steps should be tried:

Keeping in mind that the most reasonable expectation for taking a test is to expect to try to demonstrate as much of what you know as you possibly can.
Reminding ourselves that a test is only one test; this is not the only one, and there will be others.
The thought of thinking of oneself in an irrational, all-or-nothing term should be avoided at all costs.
A reward should be designated for after the test, so there's something to look forward to. Whether it be going to a movie, going out to eat, or simply visiting friends, schedule it in advance, and do it no matter what result is expected on the exam.

Test-takers should also keep in mind that the basics are some of the most important things, even beyond anti-anxiety techniques and studying. Never neglect the basic social, emotional and biological needs, in order to try to absorb information. In order to best achieve, these three factors must be held as just as important as the studying itself.

Study Steps

Remember the following important steps for studying:

Maintain healthy nutrition and exercise habits. Continue both your recreational activities and social pass times. These both contribute to your physical and emotional well being.
Be certain to get a good amount of sleep, especially the night before the test, because when you're overtired you are not able to perform to the best of your best ability.
Keep the studying pace to a moderate level by taking breaks when they are needed, and varying the work whenever possible, to keep the mind fresh instead of getting bored.
When enough studying has been done that all the material that can be learned has been learned, and the test taker is prepared for the test, stop studying and do something relaxing such as listening to music, watching a movie, or taking a warm bubble bath.

There are also many other techniques to minimize the uneasiness or apprehension that is experienced along with test anxiety before, during, or even after the examination. In fact, there are a great deal of things that can be done to stop anxiety from interfering with lifestyle and performance. Again, remember that anxiety will not be eliminated entirely, and it shouldn't be. Otherwise that "up" feeling for exams would not exist, and most of us depend on that sensation to perform better than usual. However, this anxiety has to be at a level that is manageable.

Of course, as we have just discussed, being prepared for the exam is half the battle right away. Attending all classes, finding out what knowledge will be expected on the exam, and knowing the exam schedules are easy steps to lowering anxiety. Keeping up with work will remove the need to cram, and efficient study habits will eliminate wasted time. Studying should be done in an ideal location for concentration, so that it is simple to become interested in the material and give it complete attention. A method such as

SQ3R (Survey, Question, Read, Recite, Review) is a wonderful key to follow to make sure that the study habits are as effective as possible, especially in the case of learning from a textbook. Flashcards are great techniques for memorization. Learning to take good notes will mean that notes will be full of useful information, so that less sifting will need to be done to seek out what is pertinent for studying. Reviewing notes after class and then again on occasion will keep the information fresh in the mind. From notes that have been taken summary sheets and outlines can be made for simpler reviewing.

A study group can also be a very motivational and helpful place to study, as there will be a sharing of ideas, all of the minds can work together, to make sure that everyone understands, and the studying will be made more interesting because it will be a social occasion.

Basically, though, as long as the test-taker remains organized and self confident, with efficient study habits, less time will need to be spent studying, and higher grades will be achieved.

To become self confident, there are many useful steps. The first of these is "self talk." It has been shown through extensive research, that self-talk for students who suffer from test anxiety, should be well monitored, in order to make sure that it contributes to self confidence as opposed to sinking the student. Frequently the self talk of test-anxious students is negative or self-defeating, thinking that everyone else is smarter and faster, that they always mess up, and that if they don't do well, they'll fail the entire course. It is important to decreasing anxiety that awareness is made of self talk. Try writing any negative self thoughts and then disputing them with a positive statement instead. Begin self-encouragement as though it was a friend speaking. Repeat positive statements to help reprogram the mind to believing in successes instead of failures.

Helpful Techniques

Other extremely helpful techniques include:

Self-visualization of doing well and reaching goals
While aiming for an "A" level of understanding, don't try to "overprotect" by setting your expectations lower. This will only convince the mind to stop studying in order to meet the lower expectations.
Don't make comparisons with the results or habits of other students. These are individual factors, and different things work for different people, causing different results.
Strive to become an expert in learning what works well, and what can be done in order to improve. Consider collecting this data in a journal.
Create rewards for after studying instead of doing things before studying that will only turn into avoidance behaviors.
Make a practice of relaxing - by using methods such as progressive relaxation, self-hypnosis, guided imagery, etc - in order to make relaxation an automatic sensation.
Work on creating a state of relaxed concentration so that concentrating will take on the focus of the mind, so that none will be wasted on worrying.
Take good care of the physical self by eating well and getting enough sleep.
Plan in time for exercise and stick to this plan.

Beyond these techniques, there are other methods to be used before, during and after the test that will help the test-taker perform well in addition to overcoming anxiety.

Before the exam comes the academic preparation. This involves establishing a study schedule and beginning at least one week before the actual date of the test. By doing this, the anxiety of not having enough time to study for the test will be automatically eliminated. Moreover, this will make the studying a much more effective experience, ensuring that the learning will be an easier process. This relieves much undue pressure on the test-taker.

Summary sheets, note cards, and flash cards with the main concepts and examples of these main concepts should be prepared in advance of the actual studying time. A topic should never be eliminated from this process. By omitting a topic because it isn't expected to be on the test is only setting up the test-taker for anxiety should it actually appear on the exam. Utilize the course syllabus for laying out the topics that should be studied. Carefully go over the notes that were made in class, paying special attention to any of the issues that the professor took special care to emphasize while lecturing in class. In the textbooks, use the chapter review, or if possible, the chapter tests, to begin your review.

It may even be possible to ask the instructor what information will be covered on the exam, or what the format of the exam will be (for example, multiple choice, essay, free form, true-false). Additionally, see if it is possible to find out how many questions will be on the test. If a review sheet or sample test has been offered by the professor, make good use of it, above anything else, for the preparation for the test. Another great resource for getting to know the examination is reviewing tests from previous semesters. Use these tests to review, and aim to achieve a 100% score on each of the possible topics. With a few exceptions, the goal that you set for yourself is the highest one that you will reach.

Take all of the questions that were assigned as homework, and rework them to any other possible course material. The more problems reworked, the more skill and confidence will form as a result. When forming the solution to a problem, write out each of the steps. Don't simply do head work. By doing as many steps on paper as possible, much clarification and therefore confidence will be formed. Do this with as many homework problems as possible, before checking the answers. By checking the answer after each problem, a reinforcement will exist, that will not be on the exam. Study situations should be as exam-like as possible, to prime the test-taker's system for the experience. By waiting to check the answers at the end, a psychological advantage will be formed, to decrease the stress factor.

Another fantastic reason for not cramming is the avoidance of confusion in concepts, especially when it comes to mathematics. 8-10 hours of study will become one hundred percent more effective if it is spread out over a week or at least several days, instead of doing it all in one sitting. Recognize that the human brain requires time in order to assimilate new material, so frequent breaks and a span of study time over several days will be much more beneficial.

Additionally, don't study right up until the point of the exam. Studying should stop a minimum of one hour before the exam begins. This allows the brain to rest and put things in their proper order. This will also provide the time to become as relaxed as possible when going into the examination room. The test-taker will also have time to eat well and eat sensibly. Know that the brain needs food as much as the rest of the body. With enough food and enough sleep, as well as a relaxed attitude, the body and the mind are primed for success.

Avoid any anxious classmates who are talking about the exam. These students only spread anxiety, and are not worth sharing the anxious sentimentalities.

Before the test also involves creating a positive attitude, so mental preparation should also be a point of concentration. There are many keys to creating a positive attitude. Should fears become rushing in, make a visualization of taking the exam, doing well, and seeing an A written on the paper. Write out a list of affirmations that will bring a feeling of confidence, such as "I am doing well in my English class," "I studied well and know my material," "I enjoy this class." Even if the affirmations aren't believed at first, it sends a positive message to the subconscious which will result in an alteration of the overall belief system, which is the system that creates reality.

If a sensation of panic begins, work with the fear and imagine the very worst! Work through the entire scenario of not passing the test, failing the entire course, and dropping out of school, followed by not getting a job, and pushing a shopping cart through the dark alley where you'll live. This will place things into perspective! Then, practice deep breathing and create a visualization of the opposite situation - achieving an "A" on the exam, passing the entire course, receiving the degree at a graduation ceremony.

On the day of the test, there are many things to be done to ensure the best results, as well as the most calm outlook. The following stages are suggested in order to maximize test-taking potential:

Begin the examination day with a moderate breakfast, and avoid any coffee or beverages with caffeine if the test taker is prone to jitters. Even people who are used to managing caffeine can feel jittery or light-headed when it is taken on a test day.
Attempt to do something that is relaxing before the examination begins. As last minute cramming clouds the mastering of overall concepts, it is better to use this time to create a calming outlook.
Be certain to arrive at the test location well in advance, in order to provide time to select a location that is away from doors, windows and other distractions, as well as giving enough time to relax before the test begins.
Keep away from anxiety generating classmates who will upset the sensation of stability and relaxation that is being attempted before the exam.
Should the waiting period before the exam begins cause anxiety, create a self-distraction by reading a light magazine or something else that is relaxing and simple.
During the exam itself, read the entire exam from beginning to end, and find out how much time should be allotted to each individual problem. Once writing the exam, should more time be taken for a problem, it should be abandoned, in order to begin another problem. If there is time at the end, the unfinished problem can always be returned to and completed.

Read the instructions very carefully - twice - so that unpleasant surprises won't follow during or after the exam has ended.

When writing the exam, pretend that the situation is actually simply the completion of homework within a library, or at home. This will assist in forming a relaxed atmosphere, and will allow the brain extra focus for the complex thinking function.

Begin the exam with all of the questions with which the most confidence is felt. This will build the confidence level regarding the entire exam and will begin a quality momentum. This will also create encouragement for trying the problems where uncertainty resides.

Going with the "gut instinct" is always the way to go when solving a problem. Second guessing should be avoided at all costs. Have confidence in the ability to do well.

For essay questions, create an outline in advance that will keep the mind organized and make certain that all of the points are remembered. For multiple choice, read every answer, even if the correct one has been spotted - a better one may exist.

Continue at a pace that is reasonable and not rushed, in order to be able to work carefully. Provide enough time to go over the answers at the end, to check for small errors that can be corrected.

Should a feeling of panic begin, breathe deeply, and think of the feeling of the body releasing sand through its pores. Visualize a calm, peaceful place, and include all of the sights, sounds and sensations of this image. Continue the deep breathing, and take a few minutes to continue this with closed eyes. When all is well again, return to the test.

If a "blanking" occurs for a certain question, skip it and move on to the next question. There will be time to return to the other question later. Get everything done that can be done, first, to guarantee all the grades that can be compiled, and to build all of the confidence possible. Then return to the weaker questions to build the marks from there.

Remember, one's own reality can be created, so as long as the belief is there, success will follow. And remember: anxiety can happen later, right now, there's an exam to be written!

After the examination is complete, whether there is a feeling for a good grade or a bad grade, don't dwell on the exam, and be certain to follow through on the reward that was promised…and enjoy it! Don't dwell on any mistakes that have been made, as there is nothing that can be done at this point anyway.

Additionally, don't begin to study for the next test right away. Do something relaxing for a while, and let the mind relax and prepare itself to begin absorbing information again.

From the results of the exam - both the grade and the entire experience, be certain to learn from what has gone on. Perfect studying habits and work some more on confidence in order to make the next examination experience even better than the last one.

Learn to avoid places where openings occurred for laziness, procrastination and day dreaming.

Use the time between this exam and the next one to better learn to relax, even learning to relax on cue, so that any anxiety can be controlled during the next exam. Learn how to relax the body. Slouch in your chair if that helps. Tighten and then relax all of the different muscle groups, one group at a time, beginning with the feet and then working all the way up to the neck and face. This will ultimately relax the muscles more than they were to begin with. Learn how to breathe deeply and comfortably, and focus on this breathing going in and out as a relaxing thought. With every exhale, repeat the word "relax."

As common as test anxiety is, it is very possible to overcome it. Make yourself one of the test-takers who overcome this frustrating hindrance.

Additional Bonus Material

Due to our efforts to try to keep this book to a manageable length, we've created a link that will give you access to all of your additional bonus material.

Please visit http://www.mometrix.com/bonus948/staarssg4write to access the information.